Restructuring for an Interdisciplinary Curriculum

Edited by John M. Jenkins
Daniel Tanner

National Association of Secondary School Principals
Reston, Virginia

© 1992
National Association of Secondary School Principals
1904 Association Drive
Reston, Virginia 22091-1537
(703) 860-0200

Executive Director: Timothy J. Dyer
Deputy Executive Director, Director of Publications: Thomas F. Koerner
Director of Research: James W. Keefe
Editor: Patricia George
Technical Editor: Eugenia Cooper Potter

ISBN 088210251-6

Contents

About the Authors

Daniel Tanner, a member of NASSP's Curriculum Council, is a distinguished professor of education at Rutgers University, New Brunswick, N.J.

Steven S. Means is the lead teacher and co-founder of the Interrelated Curriculum at Sammamish High School, Bellevue, Washington.

Richard Lear is the senior researcher for school design for the Coalition of Essential Schools, Brown University, Providence, R.I.

Dustin Peters is a member of NASSP's Curriculum Committee and the principal of Elizabethtown (Pa.) High School. The school is affiliated with the Coalition of Essential Schools.

Donald Hayes is the senior publishing teacher, **Sue Ellen Hogan** is the principal of the Clement McDonough City Magnet School, Lowell, Mass., and **Thomas Malone** is the program facilitator at the same school.

Gerald Krumbein is principal at Landels School in Mountainview, Calif. **Suzanne R. Krumbein** is a librarian at Hillview Middle School in Menlo Park, Calif.

Andrew Alghren is the associate director of Project 2061 for the American Association for the Advancement of Science.

John Ramsey is an assistant professor in the department of curriculum and instruction at the University of Houston, Texas.

Margaret Earley recently retired as the chair, department of curriculum and instruction, College of Education, University of Florida, Gainesville. She also headed the Florida Writing Project.

John M. Jenkins, a member of NASSP's Curriculum Council, is director of the P. K. Yonge Laboratory School, University of Florida, Gainesville.

Preface

This publication has been prepared at the request of NASSP's Curriculum Committee, composed of practicing secondary school principals from various regions of the nation. It has become increasingly evident to educators that the extended period of curriculum fundamentalism ("back-to-basics") has left the schools with a narrow-minded and fragmented curriculum. Recent developments indicate clearly the need for an integrated core curriculum to meet the function of general education in a free and multicultural society. Growing recognition is being given to the need for the rising generation to understand the interconnectedness of knowledge and to develop the capability of applying this knowledge to the solution of real-life problems.

The introductory chapter not only provides a perspective of past efforts and accomplishments to develop a sense of balance and coherence in the secondary school curriculum, but shows how school administrators and teachers need to build upon that knowledge in the light of contemporary needs. Persistent danger signals are identified in the struggle for curriculum articulation and renewal as we move toward the new century.

Chapter 2 is a teacher's account of how the modest and beginning efforts of four colleagues and their assistant principal resulted in an interrelated curriculum that has grown in only a few years to involve most of the ninth-grade students and faculty, with ramifications throughout the four-year curriculum of a high school. The account is testimony to the capability of teachers with the support of their principal and assistant principal, to conduct action or developmental research for curriculum renewal.

In Chapter 3 descriptions are given of curriculum renewal efforts at three contrasting secondary schools that are among the more than 100 schools nationwide connected with the Coalition of Essential Schools. Chapter 4 presents an account of interdisciplinary team teaching at another high school affiliated with the Coalition.

The curriculum of a "micro-society" magnet school (K-8) serving a multicultural population is described in Chapter 5. In Chapter 6, a case study of an integrated block-time core program in a middle school is reported.

The widely heralded *Project 2061: Science for All Americans*, sponsored by the American Association for the Advancement of Science, is described briefly in Chapter 7. In contradistinction to the national discipline-centered projects in the wake of the cold war and space race, Project 2061 is interdisciplinary (K-12) and designed to reveal the interconnectedness of the sciences and mathematics and their significance to technology and society. Chapter 8 provides a detailed account of interdisciplinary approaches to curriculum design and development through environmental education (K-12), featuring students' engagement in problem solving.

"Writing across the curriculum" is the focus of Chapter 9. The role of the secondary school principal in ensuring the success of a curriculum-wide writing program is examined in some detail.

The final chapter discusses the significance of the contemporary rediscovery of the need for an integrated curriculum. The common threads of the various chapters in this publication are identified along with the implications for the learner, the school, and society.

The editors hope that principals and their teachers will find this publication useful as a source of ideas for faculty study and discussion, and for possible adaptation to local needs in the continual effort for curriculum renewal.

JMJ
DT

Chapter 1

Synthesis Versus Fragmentation: The Way Out of Curriculum Confusion

Daniel Tanner

In belated recognition that the curriculum retrenchment of "back-to-basics" has failed, there is growing realization of the need for concerted curriculum renewal. The success of current efforts at curriculum renewal will depend greatly on whether school leaders learn why the failure of curriculum retrenchment was inevitable, seek to develop an articulated and enriched curriculum, and strive to build upon the vast body of research literature on curriculum articulation or synthesis. What does history teach us about the vagaries of curriculum integration?

A Persistent Problem

An articulated and enriched curriculum to meet the common and diversified needs of a polyglot pupil population in the secondary school has been a persistent problem throughout this century. This need is no less crucial today than after World War I when the Commission on the Reorganization of Secondary Education issued its landmark *Cardinal Principles* report (1918). This report signaled a veritable revolutionary transformation of the American secondary school and the curriculum.

In the nineteenth century, vast industrial growth gave impetus to the movement for universal public elementary education to provide the rising generation of workers with the fundamental skills required for their jobs (Bernal, 1971). The masses were to be provided a cheap curriculum for "basic literacy," while the privileged enjoyed a full and enriched curriculum.

Early in the century, John Dewey observed that when efforts were made to enrich the curriculum for the masses, these efforts were dismissed by the more privileged as "fads and frills" who were well aware "that their own children would be able to get the things they protest against" (Dewey, 1916).

1

Prototype of American Democracy

Immediately after World War I, enormous pressures were exerted to create a dual system of secondary education patterned after the European tradition. However, embracing the powerful rationale of the *Cardinal Principles* report, our nation opted for a uniquely American unitary school structure through the coeducational comprehensive high school—the cosmopolitan school embracing all curricula. "In short," declared the report, "the comprehensive school is the prototype of a democracy in which various groups have a degree of self-consciousness as groups and yet are federated into a larger whole through the recognition of common interests and ideals. Life in such a school is a natural and valuable preparation for life in a democracy" (p.26).

Recognizing that the curriculum in such a school would need to be diversified while also providing for a sense of unity in a cosmopolitan pupil population, the framers of the *Cardinal Principles* report envisioned the curriculum as structured around a core of "constants" for all students, coupled with diversified studies or "variables" to meet individual differences.

At the same time, the report warned against tracking, attacked the doctrine that the traditional academic curriculum is the only acceptable preparation for college, and contended that the pursuit of vocational studies in high school should not be seen as a deterrent to the pursuit of higher education. "In view of the important role of secondary education," stated the report, "it follows that higher institutions of learning are not justified in maintaining entrance requirements and examinations of a character that handicap the secondary school in discharging its proper functions in a democracy" (pp. 19-20).

Common and Diversified Needs

In calling for a common core of "constants," the authors of the *Cardinal Principles* report made it clear that the core would not simply be a list of traditional departmentalized academic subjects, but would be articulated to meet the democratizing function of education. This would require special precautions against allowing the departmentalized subject structure of the high school to determine the objectives and functions of education. Instead, the objectives and functions of education should determine the organizational structure of the school and the curriculum.

In this connection it was pointed out that when "the only basis upon which a high school is organized is that of the subjects of study, each department being devoted to some particular subject, there will result an over-valuation of the importance of subjects as such, and the tendency will be for each teacher to regard his function merely that of leading the pupils to master a particular subject" (p. 27).

The ensuing decades up to World War II witnessed unprecedented efforts in curriculum reconstruction in the secondary school and college to meet the common and differentiated needs of a cosmopolitan student population as the United States led the way in embracing the ideal of universal secondary education.

The great educational transformation through the upward extension of educational opportunity required a great curriculum transformation. Progressivist-experimentalist educators held that the tradition of *basic education* or *literacy education* for the masses and *liberal* education for the privileged was untenable in a democracy.

The Idea and Practice of General Education

As a consequence, the idea of *general education* (not to be confused with the general curriculum track) gained great impetus in the quest for a core curriculum to provide for a common universe of discourse, understanding, and competence required of all citizens in a free society (Harvard Committee, 1945). It was becoming increasingly clear that the fragmented subject curriculum merely perpetuated the isolation of knowledge and was inadequate to the task of building a meaningful common core of learning.

The proliferation of segmental subjects was countered by the creation of broad fields and combined fields. Progressivist-experimentalist educators devised various new curricular designs to combat teacher isolation and to provide for curricular correlation and synthesis. Efforts were made not only to correlate subjects that until then had been treated in isolation, but to develop thematic and life-related, problem-focused studies that cut across the traditional subject boundaries.

Leading progressivist-experimentalist schools sought to organize the learning experiences in the new curricular designs to foster reflective or critical thinking. Unprecedented efforts were undertaken to systematically evaluate the outcomes of the experimental designs for general education and to challenge the traditional dominance of the colleges over the secondary-school curriculum (Aikin, 1942; French, 1957).

The Eight-Year Study (1933-1941), one of the largest-scale longitudinal investigations ever undertaken in the field of education, involved comparison populations and revealed that the traditional college-preparatory curriculum was not the best way to prepare students for college. The participating colleges reported that the students from high schools having more integrative curricular designs were more successful in college than their peers who had completed a traditional college-preparatory curriculum (Aikin, 1942).

Despite the endorsement of the findings of the study by the Association of American Colleges, the advent of World War II blunted the impact of the study. In the face of the mobilization emergency, the high schools curtailed their curricular experimentation, established double-shifts to accommodate enrollment pressures, limited facilities as school construction came to a virtual halt, and devised shortened and accelerated avenues to graduation to meet the nation's emergency manpower needs.

Counterreactions

The vast requirements for school construction following World War II gave renewed impetus to the tax conservatives who favored curtailment to the cheap curriculum of basics in the elementary school and the traditional academic subjects in the secondary school. The rise of McCarthyism produced a new wave of censorship of curricular materials and widespread avoidance of controversial issues in the curriculum.

The cold war and space race were accompanied by demands from varied quarters that we restructure our schools along the divided and selective lines of European nations and that we abandon the comprehensive high school. In the words of Admiral Rickover, "we no longer have a choice between efficient education—that is, separate schools above the elementary levels—and pure 'democratic' education which insists on the inefficient time-wasting comprehensive high school. We must opt for efficiency" (1963, p. 89).

Fortunately, a single report by James B. Conant on the American high school (1959) upheld our unitary school structure and the comprehensive high school at a time when other democratic nations were beginning to move toward the comprehensive model as a means of extending educational opportunity to the rising generations.

Nationalizing Influences

Nevertheless, the "Soviet challenge" of the cold war and space race witnessed unprecedented federal funding for curriculum reform in the elementary and secondary school, giving priority to the sciences and mathematics. The knowledge specialists in the university proceeded to embrace the discipline-centered doctrine of knowledge purity and abstraction as they promoted their own disciplines in isolation of the wider world of knowledge and action. They overlooked, ignored, or even dismissed the most fundamental factors in the educative process, namely:

- The nature, needs, and interests of the learner
- The significance of practical application of knowledge in ordinary life
- The function of the curriculum in developing an enlightened citizenry in a free society (Dewey, 1902, pp. 4-8)

In embracing "disciplinarity" as the ruling doctrine for curriculum development, emphasis was given to specialized knowledge to the neglect of knowledge synthesis and general education. Not only did the curriculum become further divided and isolated into discrete disciplines, but the priority given to the sciences and mathematics resulted in a new knowledge hierarchy with the accompanying problem of curriculum imbalance.

In the aftermath of the "new math," the "new physics," the "new chemistry," and the bandwagon of other national discipline-centered projects led by university scholar-specialists, it was discovered that students lacked the ability to make relevant knowledge applications. Moreover, in ignoring the other fundamental factors, it was found that the national goal of producing more physical scientists and applied mathematicians through the national curriculum reforms had backfired as fewer students went on to major in these fields in college despite the mushrooming college enrollments (Ellis, 1967).

Appraising the national discipline-centered curriculum projects of the 1950s and 1960s, the director of the Oak Ridge National Laboratory observed, "The professional purists, representing the spirit of the fragmented, research-oriented university, took over the curriculum reforms, and by their diligence and aggressiveness, created puristic monsters" (Weinberg, 1967, pp. 153-154).

The late Richard Feynman, Nobel laureate in physics, described the "new math" as "an abstraction from the real world . . . used by pure mathematicians in their more subtle and difficult analyses, and used by nobody else" as he went on to criticize the "new math" as "full of such nonsense" (1965).

Demand for "Relevance"

As educators were beginning to awaken to the need for a redesigned curriculum to provide for synthesis and balance, the shock waves of student protest and disruption struck the college campuses in reflection of the civil-rights movement and the Vietnam war. The great prospects of the war on poverty were virtually dashed by the war in Vietnam, as promising federal educational programs for disadvantaged children and youth were reduced to relatively modest goals.

In response to the student demand for "relevance" in the college curriculum, the colleges took the path of least resistance. Instead of restructuring the undergraduate curriculum to provide for a coherent program of general education, the colleges simply instituted a proliferation of new courses on virtually every topic that was deemed "relevant." Students were allowed increased elective options in place of general education. At the same time, the specialized curricula in the traditional departmental major fields remained virtually undisturbed.

As the college-student disruption filtered down into the high school, the response was to imitate the colleges by introducing more electives on *au courant* topics. The consequence was the further fragmentation of the curriculum and the failure to address the need for curriculum balance and synthesis.

Although the proponents of the new humanities courses in the high schools claimed that these courses provided for interdisciplinary studies, in many schools the student enrollments in the humanities courses and the black studies courses reflected the social divisions of the wider society. The need to "humanize" the schools and develop interdisciplinary curricular designs was discussed, but no concerted efforts were made in these directions in the face of the easier path of special-interest electives.

Retrenchment

The 1970s witnessed a counterreaction of educational retrenchment. National reports on educational reform were attacking the high school for its increased holding power, contending that most adolescents did not belong in high school and that the high school curriculum be reduced mainly to academic studies (National Commission on Reform of Secondary Education, 1973; Panel on Youth, 1974; National Panel on High School, 1976).

Strangely, some of the radical school critics and gurus of the counterculture of the 1960s were taking the position that the high school cater exclusively to academically oriented youth while leaving other youngsters to find other means of making their way into society, or by separating them from their peers through a divided system of academic and vocational schools (Friedenberg, 1967; Goodman, 1970). The federal Vocational Education

Act of 1963 had indeed provided the means for such separation on either a full-time or shared-time basis in area or county vocational schools.

The counterreaction of curricular retrenchment of the 1970s was heralded by the slogan, "Back-to-Basics." Worksheets and workbooks proliferated. Textbooks were "dumbed down" to the neglect of ideas and higher-order thinking (California Curriculum Commission, 1984).

Expenditures for books and other curricular materials declined by 50 percent over a 17-year period so they amounted to only 0.7 percent of the operating costs of schools (National Commission on Excellence, 1983). To meet the pressures of minimum-competency and standardized-achievement tests, teachers were expected to "teach-the-test."

One of the unanticipated consequences of the "back-to-basics" retrenchment (which should have been anticipated) was the decline in writing ability and thinking ability. Whereas the great American tradition of pragmatism and experimentalism had embraced the idea of social progress or progressive social improvement through the means of public education, leading professional education journals were featuring articles on "managing education's era of decline" (Divoky, 1979). Nevertheless, the American public's belief in education remained unshaken as succeeding generations of parents sought to secure increased educational opportunity for their children.

New Nationalizing Influences

The decade of the 1980s was marked by a new nationalistic wave for educational reform reminiscent of the cold war and space race. But this time the priority to be given to the sciences and mathematics was directed no longer at the "Soviet challenge" but at the "Japanese challenge."

In apparent contradiction, the national reports on educational reform blamed the schools for the decline of U.S. dominance over world industrial markets in the face of Japanese competition, while at the same time the reports contended that our schools should be revamped to meet our future as a service economy rather than a production economy (National Commission on Excellence, 1983). Ironically, no criticisms were leveled at the shortcomings of our industrial, business, and political leadership, or at our institutions of higher education. Paradoxically, the call was for adopting the managerial techniques of American business in administering our schools.

"Schools of Choice"

The 1980s also found renewed support for restructuring the schools and establishing special-interest schools. Whereas the federal efforts to promote school vouchers and alternative schools had failed to capture public support during the 1970s, the new label of the 1980s, "schools of choice," proved to be more attractive.

Proponents of "schools of choice" were neglecting the danger signals of creating a divided and fragmented system of schools geared to serving special-interest constituencies (Raywid, 1990). They failed to recognize the historic struggle, beginning early in our century, for the creation of a unitary school system as opposed to the divided system of the Old World.

The Comprehensive High School and the Comprehensive Curriculum

Historically, the comprehensive high school had been opposed from its inception by those from the political right. However, by the 1980s it was being attacked not only by political conservatives, but also by those who viewed themselves as advocates of educational opportunity. In attacking the comprehensive high school, they revised our history to portray this unique American institution as an instrument of social division. They confused pupil grouping with tracking and erroneously held that a diversified curriculum was synonymous with tracking (Oakes, 1985). They saw the high school as appropriately limited to an academic curriculum for all youth.

In effect, they failed to recognize general education as the unitary function of a comprehensive curriculum in which students would also have the opportunity to meet their varied needs through diversified prevocational and vocational studies, college-preparatory studies, exploratory studies, enrichment studies, and special-interest studies. They took no cognizance of the rich literature in the curriculum field showing how general education and the diversified studies that comprise the curriculum can be treated in their vital interdependence.

In the metaphor of the Harvard Report (1945), general education should be seen as the palm of the hand, with the five fingers of diversified studies stretching out beyond the common core (p. 102). As an illustration of this vital interdependence, many a scientist, engineer, and skilled tradesperson has commented on the great usefulness of the studio arts in the school curriculum in developing their ability to make line drawings, sketches, and diagrams so essential to their professional work, not to mention the value derived from these arts in general education, enrichment education, and developing special interests and talents. The same applies to the value of the industrial arts which also provide a laboratory for cooperative learning. In the words of the Harvard Report:

> The manipulation of objects, the use of tools, and the construction of simple apparatus all are required for entry into the world of experimentation. Even the pure mathematician is greatly aided by shop experience; the forms, contours, and interrelations of three-dimensional objects provide a stimulus and satisfaction not to be achieved altogether within the limits of plane diagrams. The lack of shop training is at present a most serious deterrent to entry into all types of technological work and to college and postgraduate training in science, medicine, and engineering (p. 160).

Persistent Danger Signals

At long last, we are witnessing a rediscovery of the need for curricular balance and unity. There is renewed recognition of the significance of critical thinking as a function of the curriculum, and of the need to develop the fundamental processes, such as writing, throughout the curriculum.

Various professional educational associations are seeking ways of regenerating the school curriculum through interdisciplinary designs directed at revealing the social significance of knowledge, such as the interfaces of science and society. There is renewed recognition that history and the social studies should not be taught apart from literature, and that mathematics should not be taught apart from the sciences or without useful application in the life of the learner (American Association for the Advancement of Science, 1989).

Nevertheless, danger signals persist. In the pursuit of academic excellence, children and youth at risk are neglected. Vocational education within the mainstream of our high schools continues to suffer from inadequate funding and recognition. Perennialists and essentialists continue to promote a narrow notion of the mission of the school as the mere transmission of basic knowledge under the rubric of "cultural literacy" (Bloom, 1987; Hirsch, 1987).

The "new basics" are being fashioned and promoted by special-interest groups in a host of fractionated forms of "literacy," reflecting the fragmentation of the curriculum and society.

For children and youth who are socioeconomically impoverished, there is the traditional "basic literacy." For all others, there is a multitude of literacies competing for a place in the congested curriculum: "cultural literacy," "computer literacy," "mathematical literacy," "scientific literacy," "economic literacy," "political literacy," "aesthetic literacy," "technological literacy," and so on.

Standardized achievement tests drive the curriculum as never before. Despite the exceedingly low validity of these tests as predictors of academic or college success, they have been promoted by the media as scientific gauges of educational failure or effectiveness.

These tests have been used by school administrators—under pressure from the media, school boards, parents, and politicians—as evidence that their own schools are above the national norms. (Most school districts can make this claim despite the statistical impossibility, simply because the norms for the tests are several years old and new norms are not available until new tests are developed.)

Teachers are pressured to teach-the-test, resulting in improved test scores, but not real gains in achievement (Linn, Grave, and Sanders, 1990; Madaus, 1988). Real achievement in education and life is based on motivation and power, not the speed and nervous energy of test-taking. Because these tests are limited to narrow segments of the school curriculum, they convey the message that only these segments really count.

Balance and Unity in the Curriculum

From our rich heritage in the curriculum field, we can solve the persistent problem of curriculum congestion, fragmentation, and isolation by assuming a more holistic rationale and drawing upon the proven practices in curriculum development, as illustrated by the following (Tanner and Tanner, 1987, pp. 517-523):

- Instead of thinking of curriculum development as merely a segmental process of adding, deleting, and revising individual courses and requirements within the departmental cocoons, it is seen as a holistic and continuous process. The focus is on the macrocurricular functions of general education or common learnings (requiring a core of unified studies for all), along with exploratory, enrichment, specialized, and special-interest studies to meet the diversified needs of a cosmopolitan student population.

- Standing interdepartmental committees are organized to address the above macrofunctions of the curriculum. The work of these committees is guided by the principle that the value of any subject or study is determined by what it contributes to other studies in the total curriculum.

- No useful purpose is served in placing students in curricular tracks. A school having a comprehensive curriculum and a cosmopolitan student population will find that students will pursue diversified studies in accordance with their perceived interests, needs, and advice from teachers, counselors, parents, and peers. The challenge is to capitalize on the cosmopolitan quality of the student population by developing a sense of unity through diversity by means of the common core of general education. The problem is not how to separate students, but how to bring them together.

- The curriculum is restructured through designs for correlated, interdisciplinary, problem-focused, and thematic studies that reveal the interdependence of knowledge and the uses of knowledge in the life of the learner and in the life of the wider society. There is a coherent curriculum in general education rather than elective requirements.

- In restructuring the curriculum, emphasis is given to idea-oriented, problem-focused studies as opposed to error-oriented teaching. The former are of interest to students from a wide range of backgrounds and abilities and are more stimulating than error-oriented approaches consisting of disjointed facts and narrow skills. Skills are best developed through meaningful and useful contexts. Facts are not synonymous with knowledge; they must be transformed into the working power of intelligence.

- The supervisory program treats curriculum, instruction, and learning as interdependent.

- The balance and coherence of the curriculum is maintained in the face of any special priorities that may be established for the school (e.g., priority given to science and mathematics is not at the expense of other studies). The curriculum is not dominated by the college-preparatory function, but is designed to meet the needs of a cosmopolitan student population.

- The responsibility for designing and developing the curriculum resides with the professional staff of the school district and school. (Although states may mandate specific subjects for high-school graduation, they do not mandate how the subjects are to be organized and treated in the curriculum.)

- Student assignments and homework stimulate interest in learning. Homework is not mechanical drudgery.

- Teacher-made tests are focused on higher-order thinking and problem solving related to life needs. These tests are used by the teacher to evaluate the teacher's success in effecting student growth.

- Standardized achievement tests are not allowed to drive the curriculum. Nor are they used for segregating or tracking students. Such tests are used appropriately for diagnostic purposes.
- The school schedule is designed to facilitate the curriculum, not to constrain it. Scheduling considerations do not result in student tracking.
- Textbooks do not determine the courses of study, but are used along with a rich variety of curricular materials, resources, projects, and other activities for productive learning.
- Teachers are free from external constraints and pressures that may lead to the censorship of the curriculum or of curricular materials, or to teacher self-imposed censorship. Teachers are free to teach so that students may be free to learn.

Past, Present, and Future

There is much to be learned from our curriculum history. Instead of following the dominant tide of the times or current cycle of educational reform, educators must build upon the best available knowledge so real progress can be made. Otherwise the schools become vulnerable to fads and to repetitive and conflicting cycles of reform and counterreform. Priority given to one area of the curriculum is taken in opposition to another area. Priority given to one pupil population is taken at the expense of another population.

American democracy requires that the widest public interest is served through the public school. In effect, as Dewey pointed out, the real essentials of the curriculum are "the things which are socially most fundamental, that is, which have to do with the experiences in which the widest groups share." Consequently, "the scheme of a curriculum must take account of the adaptation of studies to the needs of existing community life; it must select with the intention of improving the life we live in common so that the future shall be better than the past" (1916, p. 225).

References

Aikin, W.A. *The Story of the Eight-Year Study*. New York: Harper & Row, 1942.

Alberty, H.B., and Alberty, E.J. *Reorganizing the High School Curriculum*, 3rd ed. New York: Macmillan, 1962.

American Association for the Advancement of Science. *Science for All Americans*; *Biological and Health Sciences*; *Mathematics*; *Physical and Information Sciences and Engineering*; *Social and Behavioral Sciences*; *Technology*. Washington, D.C.: The Association, 1989.

Bernal, J.D. *Science in History*, Vol. 4. Cambridge, Mass.: M.I.T., 1971.

Bloom, A. *The Closing of the American Mind*. New York: Simon and Schuster, 1987.

California Curriculum Commission. *Science Framework Addendum*. Sacramento: California State Department of Education, 1984.

Commission on the Reorganization of Secondary Education. *Cardinal Principles of Secondary Education*. Washington, D.C.: U.S. Bureau of Education, 1918.

Conant, J.B. *Education in a Divided World*. Cambridge, Mass.: Harvard University Press, 1949.

_____. *The American High School Today*. New York: McGraw-Hill, 1959.

_____. "The Comprehensive High School." In *High School 1980*, edited by A.C. Eurich. New York: Pitman, 1970.

Dewey, J. *The School and Society*. Chicago: University of Chicago, 1899.

_____. *The Child and the Curriculum*. Chicago: University of Chicago, 1902.

_____. *Democracy and Education*. New York: Macmillan, 1916.

_____. "Learning to Earn." *School and Society* 5(1917): 332.

_____. *How We Think*, rev. ed. Lexington, Mass.: D.C. Heath, 1933.

Divoky, D. "Burden of the Seventies: The Management of Decline." *Phi Delta Kappan* 61(1979): 87-91.

Educational Policies Commission. *Education for ALL American Youth—A Further Look*. Washington, D.C.: The Commission, 1952.

Ellis, S.D. "Enrollment Trends." *Physics Today* 20(1967): 77.

Feynman, R.P. "New Textbooks for the New Mathematics." *Engineering and Science* 28(1965): 13-15

French, W. *Behavioral Goals of General Education in High School*. New York: Russell Sage Foundation, 1957.

Friedenberg, E.Z. *Growing Up in America*. New York: Vintage, 1967.

Giles, H.H. et al. *Exploring the Curriculum*. New York: Harper & Row, 1942.

Goodman, P. *New Reformation*. New York: Random House, 1970.

Harvard Committee. *General Education in a Free Society*. Cambridge, Mass.: Harvard, 1945.

Hirsch, E.D., Jr. *Cultural Literacy*. New York: Random House, 1987.

Linn, R.; Grave, M.E.; and Sanders, N. "Comparing State and District Test Results to National Norms." Los Angeles, Calif.: Center for Research on Evaluation, Standards, and Student Testing, UCLA, 1990.

Madaus, George F. "The Influence of Testing on the Curriculum." In *Critical Issues in Curriculum*, edited by L.N. Tanner. National Society for the Study of Education, 87th Yearbook, Pt. I. Chicago: University of Chicago, 1988.

National Commission on Excellence in Education. *A Nation at Risk: The Imperative for Educational Reform*. Washington, D.C.: U.S. Department of Education, 1983.

National Commission on the Reform of Secondary Education. *The Reform of Secondary Education*. New York: McGraw-Hill, 1973.

National Panel on High School and Adolescent Education. *The Education of Adolescents*. Washington, D.C.: U.S. Office of Education, 1976.

Oakes, J. *Keeping Track: How High Schools Structure Inequality*. New Haven: Yale, 1985.

Panel on Youth of the President's Science Advisory Committee. *Youth: Transition to Adulthood*. Chicago: University of Chicago, 1974.

Raywid, M.A. "Is There a Case for Choice?" *Educational Leadership* 48(1990): 4-12.

Rickover, H.G. *American Education—A National Failure*. New York: Dutton, 1963.

Tanner, D. "Splitting Up the School System." *Phi Delta Kappan* 61(1979): 92-97.

_____. "The Curriculum Frontier." *Social Education* 54 (1990): 195-97.

Tanner, D., and Tanner, L.N. *Curriculum Development: Theory Into Practice*, 2nd ed. New York: Macmillan, 1980.

_____. *Supervision in Education: Problems and Practices*. New York: Macmillan, 1987.

_____. *History of the School Curriculum*. New York: Macmillan, 1990.

Weinberg, A.M. *Reflections on Big Science*. Cambridge, Mass.: The M.I.T. Press, 1967.

Chapter 2

The Interrelated Curriculum

Steven S. Means

Education takes place inside students. This education is interdisciplinary and integrated whether or not that is the explicit goal of teachers or the school system. Students relate each subject and each experience to their previous learning, to their personal lives, and to the world around them. A teacher (or a school system) can choose to directly aid each student in this process by providing a curriculum that expects meaning in relationships, in content, and in experience. Relationships can be established among all participants. Teachers can work together in various groupings. Students can help define curriculum.

Michael F. Connelly (1988) points out that "When we set our imaginations free from the narrow notion that a course of study is a series of textbooks or a specific outline of topics to be covered and objectives to be attained, broader and more meaningful notions emerge. A curriculum can become one's life course of action." When the curriculum is adjusted to the participating students' and teachers' life courses of action, relationships enhance and give meaning to the educational process. When a faculty works together to develop relational enhancements among the activities that go on in the classroom, education becomes more powerful and meaningful.

The Start

The seeds of improvement abound in every school and in every classroom. The nurturing soil, sun, and water come in many forms, but all must be present for improvement to sprout. Teachers with the inspiration need time, funds, administrative direction, and community support in addition to willing students. The development of the Interrelated Curriculum at Sammamish High School has been surrounded by many seasons of support. The sun did not shine every day nor did it rain every time it was needed.

It is important to credit the efforts that helped turn inspiration into education.

Sammamish is a comprehensive high school in Bellevue, Wash., with an enrollment of 1,400 students in grades 9 through 12. In early 1985, the assistant principal (current principal), Mary Lou Johnson, obtained a grant to support interested teachers in forming an alternate approach to the education of our students. The narrower task was to add a global component to our teaching efforts. The broader task was to provide Sammamish students with an education appropriate to the requirements of an increasingly global society.

The grant enabled almost half the 80 faculty members to discuss the possibilities of enhancing the curriculum through interdisciplinary efforts. They were influenced by the well-expressed concerns of Edward de Bono (1973) and Walter Parker (1990) that critical thinking skills should permeate the curriculum. They wished to expand the curriculum with practical applications of skills and knowledge. They felt that students needed help in integrating the increasing body of information into a coherent whole. These and many more theories and dreams were shared.

The current principal's interest in the Interrelated Curriculum has been unfaltering. First-year interdisciplinary (ID) teachers were provided an extra common planning period during which they developed curriculum based on emerging student needs, counseled students, and monitored the directions the program was taking. During the second year the lead teacher received one extra free period to coordinate the program and to establish a working relationship with local community resources, the University of Washington, and area theaters. In subsequent years, teachers within the program were given a common planning period. Additional funding was obtained. From the start, the former principal Karin Cathey, the district administrators, and the Bellevue School Board supported the effort.

Change is particularly difficult to support in positive environments. Our clichés defend our inertia: *If it ain't broke don't fix it.* The investments teachers have in training, professional experience, and personal security lead them quite reasonably to support the status quo. The initial development of our Interrelated Curriculum was one expression of a widespread desire to seek solutions to our educational challenges. Our staff applied for a grant under Washington State's Schools for the 21st Century program. This grant has supported teacher efforts for six years with 10 extra day's pay and $50,000 per year for materials and new learning experiences for students. University of Washington professors Walter Parker and Nathalie Gehrke also provided initial and ongoing support for Sammamish interdisciplinary efforts.

The staff chose four teachers to begin using the new methods at the start of the 1986-87 school year. All agreed to avoid reinventing the wheel. Help and suggestions were sought. Professor Gehrke provided personal guidance and had her university seminar students search the existing literature for models of high school programs that integrated the teaching of the core subjects of mathematics, science, language arts, and social studies.

In late July of 1986, the four pilot teachers met with the university researchers to learn that, despite dozens of references to integrated curriculum, there were few recorded models and not even one lesson plan deemed appropriate for the high school level. Evidence existed of a substantial amount of team teaching between and among various subjects, but nothing that focused on the learner and the holistic integration of learning. Five weeks remained before the selected students would come for the new classes.

Guiding Principles and Goals

The original four teachers agreed on five guiding principles:

- Any innovation could not negatively affect their students. A student should be able to enter or leave the interdisciplinary program at any time without too much difficulty.
- Efforts to integrate curricula should never be artificial.
- The program should support the many goals the faculty committee had agreed upon.
- The work should be professionally rewarding.
- It all should be fun.

The faculty committee agreed upon the following goals:

1. Emphasize writing skills in all subjects.
2. Provide a friendly transition to high school for incoming students.
3. Communicate well with parents.
4. Teach critical thinking skills.
5. Teach study and learning skills.
6. Develop each student's commitment to the community.
7. Extend activities of the classroom to the school, home, and community.
8. Develop teaching strategies that increase each teacher's job satisfaction.
9. Monitor student progress cooperatively; teachers work together.
10. Provide a wide variety of adult role models, of adults seen as learners.
11. Foster and monitor each student's emotional and personal growth.
12. Provide expectations that are consistent across the disciplines.

Out of these common objective have come integrated lessons and classroom procedures, special projects, and community activities for a pilot program with ninth graders that has become an ongoing program for all students with significant ramifications for improving the total school curriculum. (See Figure 1 for the current Sammamish Vision Statement.)

Figure 1

The faculty goals that guided the original team of four ID teachers six years ago developed into a **vision statement** for the whole school:

Sammamish is commited to creating an environment in which ALL students can learn. To this end, we believe that students should posses the following skills and characteristics as graduates from Sammamish High School:

1. Students will develop mental, physical, and emotional health for the total person, becoming aware of mind, body, feelings, spirit, and imagination. This includes valuing oneself and accepting differences.

2. Students will develop the ability and desire to be lifelong learners who perceive change as a natural part of life and use change to their advantage.

3. Students will demonstrate the ability to solve problems, reason logically and creatively through the application of appropriate thinking skills.

4. Students will perceive that knowledge is interrelated rather than segmented. They will experience learning through activities that draw from knowledge in a variety of subject areas.

5. Students will acquire a thorough understanding of the interdependence and interrelatedness of the diverse peoples and nations in the world and of the natural, human, and man-made forces that affect us all.

6. Students will develop a community service commitment and be interested in making positive changes in the world.

7. Students will acquire a basic cadre of essential knowledge and aesthetic experience.

8. Students will demonstrate effective verbal, written, visual, and listening communication skills.

9. Students will use technology to enhance their lives and be able to understand and analyze the implications of technology in their lives.

10. Students will be given the opportunity to demonstrate skills and knowledge in a variety of processes and models.

11. Students will take the initiative and responsibility in making all the above a reality.

The Challenge of Change

Substantial changes within a school affect all programs. During each of the six years that we have worked on interdisciplinary enhancements to student experiences at Sammamish there have been reports of scheduling conflicts, unequal work loads, funding difficulties, and philosophical and professional differences. Each year the staff is better able to deal with scheduling problems. But problems continue to exist with class size. Indeed, Interdisciplinary-Block classes have been a little larger than the school average.

Not all Sammamish teachers feel that the Interrelated Curriculum (and the Interdisciplinary Block) is positive. Some believe that the program is another step toward weakening the traditional disciplines. Evaluation has been quite thorough and indications are that students learn substantially more of the traditional subjects when they are taught within the Interdisciplinary Program. Not all regular teachers, however, have used the same pre and post-tests as ID Block teachers. Normative comparisons cover the effectiveness of previous teaching by ID Block teachers, evidence of growth of individual students, and more general statistical comparisons. Anecdotal analyses as well as input and assessment from students and parents have indicated strong approval. As part of her graduate work in progress at the Seattle University, Marcia Zervis used "Action Research" (Hopkins, 1985) to provide our site-based management team with independent information.

Occasional attempts to modify or reduce the Interrelated Curriculum have been turned back by a strong coalition of parents, students, and staff. Although the Interrelated Curriculum does not yet solve all the problems perceived by the staff, it receives high marks. Pre-tests in mathematics show lower incoming skills for students each year, but post-tests reflect unprecedented growth and much above average competence in algebra and geometry. More students are going on to higher levels of math and science after experience in the Interrelated Curriculum. ID students show strong scores in science, increased interest in current events, and significantly greater participation in community and school service.

Communication with the Staff

Interdisciplinary teachers have provided regular reports and demonstrations for the rest of the Sammamish staff and encouraged them to participate in some way during the year. The following excerpt is taken from a 1987 memo that helped us develop a working definition of interdisciplinary education.

It is important not to quibble over words; it is important to describe and contrast. The term "interdisciplinary" is currently being used in two very different contexts. It is used casually to relabel teaching strategies that have been in practice here for some time. It is used more narrowly by ID Program teachers to define and enhance our understanding of new educational processes.

The ID Program's working definition of *interdisciplinary education* is quite distinct from other definitions you might encounter. The first distinction is our holistic focus on the processes occurring in the student; that is, our interest in the daily struggle of our students to integrate particularized bits of learning into a valuable education. Our goal is to directly and consistently help the student put the pieces together.

A working definition can be an action item that acquires meaning through application. In this spirit, the ID Program teachers spend little time debating the terminology and prefer to attempt the task.

1. Develop an understanding of each student as a learner and as a person. Share the points of view of the cooperating teachers. Discuss curricular goals with each student. Agree on strategies to work toward realizing the goals.
2. Arrange school experiences that relate to real world experiences and student goals.
3. Ask students to extend and integrate their school learning with regular and diverse experiences in the community.
4. Teach thinking, learning, and study skills.
5. Use any combination of subject-based skills in any particular lesson. Cover all basic student learning objectives (SLOs) defined by the district or state for this level. Place emphasis on mastering and using the traditional basic skills.
6. Integrate physical activities into the curriculum.
7. Seek common themes that are worth pursuing not just in classrooms, but also in the halls, at home, at work, and at play.

It is the education happening inside each learner and teacher that is at the center of our working definition of *interdisciplinary education*.

Structure and Methods of the Interrelated Curriculum

During recent years, approximately 180 students, two of every three, have participated in the Ninth-Grade Interdisciplinary Program. Students in the 1991-92 ID Block received traditional credit in language arts, social studies, science, and computer skills. In earlier years, ID students also received credit for mathematics and physical education.

Our ID Block schedule supports a range of learning experieces. (See Figure 2.) The ID students participate in many experiences and tasks typically absent or minimally present in the traditional classroom. These include field trips, writing assignments from multiple points of view on multiple subjects, technical writing, community service, coordination of study loads (we avoid testing in several areas on the same day), special weekly group meetings, direct teaching, and regular application of critical thinking, study, and learning skills. Questions of ethics are addressed by faculty and students in writing and in discussion. The importance and impact of current local and global events are addressed each week. A personal-choice curriculum is approached through individual counseling, large group speakers, drama productions, and academic analysis. Students learn how to be an audience for live drama performances produced here at school and in area theaters. They go behind the scenes to learn about staging, sound, and lighting.

The teachers in the program are free to change the time, length, frequency, and content of individaul and group lessons. The total time traditionally allocated to the source subjects is assigned at (ID Block) teacher discretion. Large-group meetings in the theater last as long as needed. Traditional class lessons may be shortened or lengthened. Activities and field trips may take place after usual school hours or on weekends. Redeveloping a salmon run in a local stream require student and teacher efforts for several weeks. An extended trip was taken to the Olympic National Park rain forests.

Parents and other community members are encouraged to work with students on extended learning opportunities. Students are expected to express the other points of view they encounter in their writings about their experiences. During the second semester students spend four hours per month in community service. Each month is a different experience. Student writing about these experiences represents perhaps the deepest and most powerful individual student learning this teacher has encountered.

All ID students share extended learning and writing assignments. Every two weeks they turn in a short paper summarizing an experience that includes at least two people's point of view. Each teacher shares equally in the ID teaching load. Science, keyboarding, physical education, and math teachers must read and react to the same amount of ID writing as English and history teachers. The experiences that students report may include visits to museums, zoos, businesses, industries, exhibits, community events,

Figure 2
Sammamish High School Year Six Schedules: 1991-92

Student Schedules		Teacher Schedules	
ID Block A	**ID Block B**	**English, Social Studies, and Science**	**Science, English, and Computer Skills**
Pd.1 ID A *(Combines English, social studies, and science)*	Pd.1 Foreign Language	Pd.1 ID A	Pd.1 Regular Course
Pd.2 ID A	Pd.2 Open (or elective)	Pd.2 ID A	Pd.2 Planning
Pd.3 ID A	Pd.3 PE	Pd.3 ID A	Pd.3 Regular Course
Pd.4 Algebra	Pd.4 Math *(Combines English and social studies, computer skills, and Northwest History)*	Pd.4 Planning	Pd.4 Planning
Pd.5 Foreign Language	Pd.5 ID B	Pd.5 Regular Courses	Pd.5 ID B
Pd.6 Open (or elective)	Pd.6 ID B	Pd.6 Planning	Pd.6 ID B
Pd.7 PE	Pd.7 ID B	Pd.7 Regular Course	Pd.7 ID B

Students may choose ID Block A or B. The two blocks support a wide range of student experiences and flexible scheduling. Sammamish has settled on three period blocks for ninth graders and an interrelated curriculum for all students.

concerts, and the viewing of certain selected TV broadcasts. Students work with their teachers to select activities that extend their experiences and learning into new arenas. Standards for writing are agreed upon across the disciplines.

At least once a week, all 180 students meet together for a large-group experience. Students are taught how to be an audience and how to profit from the various events. One week the focus might be on the environment, another week on crime, yet another week on personal, moral, and ethical choices. Special dramatic performances occur monthly. These include student productions by Sammamish and other schools as well as professional performances supported by grant monies.

Our students participate in the University of Washington's Meany Theater World Dance program, which brings university and professional dancers to the school and includes a field trip to the university campus for special matinee performances. Large-group and individual class activities support field trips to the special exhibits that have come to the Seattle area during the past several years.

In support of a visit by the North American Indian Dance Ensemble, our technology teacher joined with an art teacher to show how available materials influenced the choices local Indians made in terms of symbols, clothing, shelter, food, ceremonies, and even weapons and religion. Similar experiences included an African musician who taught the students native dance movements and a couple from the Nikolais dance troupe who showed students how to expand the dance experience with ribbons, cloth, light, and abstract objects.

A considerable curriculum of interrelated experiences has been developed. Some of these transcend normal subject matter boundaries and some support two traditional subjects. For example, the study of Robert Heinlein's science-fiction novel, **Tunnel in the Sky**, was enhanced by studying the applied technology needed to survive in new environments, the needs for law, government, and ethics in an independent society, the mathematical implications of growth patterns, the human needs for diversion and entertainment, and the functions of effective leadership.

Monitoring student learning during the reading of **Tunnel in the Sky** revealed areas of student strength (factual recall) and areas of weakness (the ability to formulate and defend judgments). This assessment led to the adoption of Edward de Bono's thinking skill material. We added the following concepts to those of de Bono's:

● The ways in which emotions and immediate experience shape a person's point of view;

- The ways in which a person's own blend of multiple intelligences (Gardner, 1983) shapes that person's focus; and
- The concept that any person may have more than one point of view and may change points of view to the surprise, but not always delight, of others.

Lessons on such topics as thinking skills are not taught exclusively by teachers in the ID Block. The principal and her assistants serve as quest teachers, as do other faculty and staff and various people from the community at large. Input from business and industry has shaped suggestions for essay writing. Students now write essays in similar styles in mathematics, science, and physical education. In addition to traditional introductions and conclusions, the body of the writing must include clear definitions, actual applications, and graphs, tables and pictures to clarify and emphasize meaning. When appropriate, the writing must include the writer's opinion or position and at least one other person's point of view. We have found that technical writing of this kind enhances the ability of students to make sense out of math lessons, to find application and meaning in scientific studies, and to see clearly the personal and cultural values of physical activities, sports and games.

Other Enhancements

The Sammamish staff offers an enhanced schedule to the entire student body during the second semester. On 8 to 12 occasions during the semester, the regular periods are expanded to 90 minutes and spread over two days. An extra period is added during which special courses and experiences are offered, such as computer communications, sculpture, and honors extensions to the established courses. (This enhanced schedule is referred to as "Flex Days.")

An "After Hours" program offers supplemental instruction ranging from tutorial help to computer use. Instructors are brought in for specialized topics of practical and immediate value. Community members are encouraged to participate in this program both as teachers and as students.

Occasional week-long events involve the whole school in the study of an era, (e.g., *Fin de Siecle - Turn of the Century*) or of an area (e.g., the Pacific Rim), or of an identified student need such as alumni careers. Activities range from costume days to sports and dance programs, theater and debate, video and music, technology and science. Local and regional businesses and agencies send materials and representatives to Sammamish to participate in and to enhance this part of our curriculum.

Sammamish offers a broad range of student activities. Participants are expected to use academic, social, and technical skills for the success of each program. Our Earth Corps group used writing and persuasion skills to obtain grants to support recycling and waste reduction. Students in art and graphics support the related publicity and educational program. Cheerleaders, musicians, and performing arts students prepare an assembly to enlist student and faculty supoort for their efforts.

Each club and activity is encouraged to develop student competence, which can be measured by beneficial changes in the general community. Students write announcements, descriptions, advertisements, brochures, and thank-you letters. They obtain advice and support from the community for their efforts. All leadership students must demonstrate competent use of basic computer skills in word processing, database management, spreadsheet accounting, and telecommunications. To do all this, students must read with full understanding, communicate with effect, and remember what is important and necessary. They learn to schedule, to delegate, to cooperate, and to complete. The student activities program is a fertile area for extended student learning.

Teachers throughout the building cooperate with each other, share expertise, and coordinate events. The drama teacher chooses productions not just for his actors but in support of goals in English and history classes. Our music teachers see their subject as part of most human events and provide support for everything from the Civil War to the Gay '90s and Turn of the Century. Physical education teachers incorporate American history in their square dance program, and global education by offering games and sports popular in other nations. They provide discussion time in their classes about topics of schoolwide, interpersonal, or even international significance.

Conclusions and the Future

Enhancements to the traditional isolated subject matter curriculum are far less difficult to make than we originally contemplated. Teachers find connections easy to make, and making adjustments to curriculum exciting. The rewards of increased student achievement and teacher sense of accomplishment supply sufficient motivation to guarantee ongoing support for integrated, interdisciplinary, extended, and applied curricula. We have not found it necessary to give up any of the proven content areas, only to teach them in relation to each other and in relation to the new topics and ideas always developing.

The Interrelated Curriculum helps students to know the relevance of their efforts to learn. Successful teachers use themselves as bridges over which they invite their students to cross; having facilitated the crossing they joyfully collapse, encouraging the students to create bridges of their own. At Sammamish High School these bridges have become multi-dimensional webs, gaining strength by being connected. And they have no need to collapse since what is learner and what is teacher are intimately interwoven.

Selected References

Buscaglia, L. *Living, Loving & Learning.* New York: Ballantine Books, 1982.

de Bono, E. "opv" CoRT THINKING. Elmsford, N.Y.: Pergamon Press, 1973.

_____. *Teaching Thinking.* New York: Penguin Books, 1982.

Connelly, F., and Clandinin, D. *Teachers as Curriculum Planners: Narratives of Experience.* New York: Teachers College Press, 1988.

Costa, I., ed. *Developing Minds.* Alexandria, Va.: Association for Supervision and Curriculum Development, 1985.

Eisner, E.W. *The Educational Imagination: On the Design and Evaluation of School Programs.* New York: Macmillan, 1991.

Gardner, H. *Frames of Mind: The Theory of Multiple Intelligences.* New York: Basic Books, 1983.

Goodlad, J.I. *A Place Called School.* New York: McGraw-Hill, 1984.

Hopkins, D. *A Teacher's Guide to Classroom Research.* Bristol, Pa.: Open University Press, 1985.

Jacobs, H.H., et al. *Interdisciplinary Curriculum: Design and Implementation.* Alexandria, Va.: Association for Supervision and Curriculum Development, 1989.

Link, F., with Walters, J.M., and Gardner, H. *Essays on the Intellect.* Alexandria, Va.: Association for Supervision and Curriculum Development, 1985.

Parker, W. *Renewing the Social Studies Curriculum.* Alexandria, Va.: Association for Supervision and Curriculum Development, 1991.

Tanner, D., and Tanner, L. *History of the School Curriculum.* New York: Macmillan, 1990.

Zervis, M. Action Research Presentation at the Spring 1991 Action Research Convention, Seattle. Unpublished manuscript, 1991.

Chapter 3

Integrated Teaching and Learning in Essential Schools

Richard Lear

Since its creation in 1984, the Coalition of Essential Schools, a partnership that includes more than 100 schools across the country and a central staff headquartered at Brown University, has been rethinking pedagogy and redesigning schools in ways that lead to improved student performance.

The Coalition, chaired by Ted Sizer, is based on the nine Common Principles (see sidebar) developed by Sizer after the completion of A Study of High Schools, which was sponsored by the National Association of Secondary School Principals and the National Association of Independent Schools.[1]

Each of the schools in the Coalition accepts the nine Common Principles as the focal point of its work. Because of Sizer's recognition that no two good schools are ever alike, each school implements the principles in ways that make most sense for that particular school and its community. As a result, no models of essential schools are available for adoption. Rather, the Coalition relies on a growing number of examples from member schools to suggest ways in which the nine Common Principles might be implemented.

With increasing frequency, those schools are including interdisciplinary or integrated teaching as part of their effort to help students learn to use their minds well. The pedagogy helps both teachers and students make the important connections among knowledge from the different academic disciplines and seems to reflect more accurately the real-world circumstances around us.

When joined with team teaching, as it most often is, integrated teaching increases the intellectual resources and support available to both students and teachers. In "Essential School" language, it provides greater personalization, helps students learn a limited area of knowledge and skills more thoroughly, gives teachers more authority over curriculum and structure, and helps teachers operate more as generalists than as subject area specialists.

This chapter contains a brief description of the diverse manner in which integrated teaching is currently used in three Essential schools: Thayer High School, the Forsyth Street site of Satellite Academy, and University Heights High School.

Each of the schools is small by contemporary American standards; the largest serves 300 students. One is rural and serves all the students in its community, while two are urban schools of choice serving students who have struggled in conventional school settings. Two of the schools have moved slowly over much of a decade to what they now call integrated teaching, while the third has considered it a basic principle of the school from its inception in 1986. Each serves a wide range of student abilities without tracking its students.

In spite of many differences—some superficial, others quite significant—the schools share a common commitment to integrated teaching that continues to push them to overcome the obstacles they face. In so doing, each school has developed different means to achieve its ends, and each provides a legitimate example for educators in schools of all sizes and circumstances who find themselves contemplating a move toward more integrated teaching.

Snapshots of the Schools

■ **Thayer Junior-Senior High School**. The approximately 300 secondary students who live in and around Winchester, a small rural community in the southwestern part of New Hampshire, attend Thayer Junior-Senior High School. The faculty and Dennis Littky, the principal, have focused intensively on improving the quality of classroom experiences for students for almost a decade as a means of raising student accomplishment and aspiration.

Thayer is a charter member of the Coalition, and the staff has achieved considerable national attention for its work in reshaping the school. Thayer's schedule is outwardly conventional: six 50-minute periods with courses that run the entire year. In practice, the schedule provides considerable flexibility for teachers. (See Figure 1 for an illustration and explanation of the ninth grade schedule.)

The staff at Thayer has begun to work with interdisciplinary instruction on a schoolwide basis for the first time this year. Each of the six grade levels

Figure 1
Thayer High School: 9th Grade Team Schedule

	Mon	Tue	Wed	Thu	Fri
7:50	Advisory Meeting	Advisory Meeting	Advisory Meeting	Advisory Meeting	Advisory Meeting
8:00 1st	Out-of-team class for 9th Grade Team teachers (4) and all ninth grade students				
8:54 2nd + 3rd	9th grade team class for 9th Grade Team teachers (4) and all ninth grade students				
10:38	Lunch	Lunch	Lunch	Lunch	Lunch
11:06 4th	9th grade team class for 9th Grade Team teachers (4) and all ninth grade students				
12:00 Band Period	Band, other activities, tutoring				
12:43 5th	9th grade team class for 9th Grade Team teachers (4) and all ninth grade students				
1:35 6th	Planning time for 9th Grade Team members (4); out-of-team class for 9th grade students				

During the Team periods, teachers may use any organizational arrangement of students, teachers, time, and space they wish. In effect, each grade level team runs a separate team schedule for its students and staff within the larger school schedule.

has a three-person team that is responsible for four academic areas. The Ninth Grade Team, for example, is responsible for math, science, social studies, and computers. (Each team has regular support, guidance, and planning assistance from a non-team teacher certified in the team's "fourth" area.)

In addition, a special education teacher or aide is a team member, and all special education students are mainstreamed. Because of scheduling constraints imposed by a small staff, students in each grade take one of their basic academic courses, as well as an elective course, outside the team structure. There are no study halls at Thayer.

Each team adopts a theme for the year. When the Ninth Grade Team chose systems as its theme, the students' first project was to study a pond as a microsystem by way of an introduction to the notion of systems and to the scientific method. The skills that were emphasized included: proper use of the scientific method; scientific identification of organisms (Latin names); proper use of microscopes, calculators, and a database; accurate diagraming of the pond; BASIC programming; research skills; and graphing skills.

During the project, students worked alone, with partners, and as part of a group, and submitted their field journals as their final exhibition. Students will study social systems, examine the interplay of biological and social systems as agricultural and nutritional systems are explored, and finally, consider global systems and human impact in the remainder of the course.

Most often, team members teach the academic area they know best, and students may receive different grades in each of the academic areas for which they receive credit.

Ninth graders know Bob Shotland as the science teacher, Julie Gainsburg as the math teacher, and Rick Durkee as the computer teacher, and they understand that all three teachers share responsibility for social studies. "Each of us still takes primary responsibility for our own discipline," says Gainsburg. "Integration (for teachers) is in knowing what others are doing and that the whole is coherent. Kids see the integration when they use materials, and data from science class, for instance, to make graphs in math."

During the team periods, teachers may use any organizational arrangement of students, teachers, time, and space they wish. Each team, in effect, runs a separate schedule, which typically varies from week to week.

For example, a week in late September consisted of the following 20 class meetings for the Ninth Grade Team: three conventional single-period regular size classes and one whole-group class (to view a film) on Monday, one double-period and two single-period regular size classes on Tuesday, Wednesday, and Thursday; and four periods of whole group classes on Friday, including an outdoor activity during which a new aspect of their project was introduced. In early November, though, only one whole-group class period was scheduled during one week.

The school's other teams make similar use of their flexibility, although all are hindered by the lack of satisfactory meeting space for large group sessions.

At the same time integrated teams were created in each grade, all special education students were mainstreamed. For special education teacher Lisen Roberts, part of the Ninth Grade Team, the decision has had enormous benefits for her students, half of whom had never been in a mainstream class before.

"I am usually in a class with the 6 of my 13 students who need the most assistance during the team periods, and I work with the other students in the resource room or during band period. I'm always part of the planning meetings, so I know what each teacher is doing. Our special ed kids are treated for the most part like other students. I provide assistance as a student seems to need it—sometimes making on-the-spot modifications, such as shortening assignments—and special ed kids are graded on the basis of their IEPs, but everything else is the same. And socially, things are much better."

While other students have accepted them as part of the class, Roberts and her teammates did note that parents of students who had formerly been in a college prep track voiced concerns about the mainstreaming.

■ **Forsyth Street**. Satellite Academy serves "at-risk" students at four sites in three different boroughs of New York City. The Forsyth Street site, located on the lower east side of Manhattan, enrolls 190 students, most of whom have previously dropped out of their high schools. The average length of enrollment for students at Forsyth Street is one-and-a-half years.

Alan Dichter, principal of Satellite Academy, notes that interdisciplinary themes emerged almost from the start of the school 19 years ago because of staff interests, and a history of creativity at the Forsyth site has supported their informal growth over the years. A more formal commitment to integrated teaching has emerged in the past five years.

Forsyth Street operates on four cycles a year, with most courses running for one cycle. The weekly schedule (Figure 2) is broken into one and two-hour blocks, with one portion of the day set aside specifically for integrated classes.

In addition to changing the structure of the day to create longer class periods as part of the move to integrated team teaching, the staff at Forsyth took two important steps, in the view of Anthony Conelli, the site coordinator. "In 1986, before the structural change, the staff took time for long discussions about how students learned and what learning was. In 1987, we met regularly to discuss team and interdisciplinary teacher, as we called it then. As we moved slowly to a purer form of integration, such topics as

Figure 2
Forsyth Street Satellite Academy Schedule*

	Mon	Tue	Wed	Thu	Fri
9:00	A	A	A	A	A
10:00	**B**: 4 integrated courses; all staff involved				
11:00	A writing lab is also taught by an English teacher during B block		C Family Group		C Family Group
12:00	Lunch				
1:00	D	D	D	D	
2:00	F	F	E	F	B

In the B block (10:00) cell:

```
B: 4 integrated courses; all staff involved
   Legend:      # tchrs              credit areas
   Course 1:      3        Eng, Am stds
   Course 2:      2        Eng, Am stds, math
   Course 3:      4        Eng, Am stds, music
   Course 4:      1        science, health
```

All staff work with students during B, C, D, E blocks and *either* A block *or* D and F blocks. Teamed staff have common planning time (6 hrs/wk). D and F block teachers may offer two separate courses or one course which utilizes both time blocks. Offering one course results in a lower overall student load.

*Forsyth uses letters to identify its periods, or "blocks," rather than numbers.

assessment, student learning habits, content, and common learning for all kids became issues we addressed."

He observes that "a good measure of integrated teaching is that it becomes difficult to say 'this amount of credit goes in this area and this amount in that,' even though the state requires us to report our courses in the usual credit rubric."[2]

Anthony also notes that "some teachers teach integrated courses on their own . . . it doesn't depend on teaming." He mentions three integrated courses currently underway at Forsyth—Latino Connections, USSR, and Human Systems—that are each taught by one teacher.

All staff members are expected to work on a team part of the day, and several staff members choose to do all their teaching in teams. The teachers enjoy teaching integrated courses as part of a team, but several, including Liz Andersen, feel that "a combination is my preference; the variety is nice, and it seems like there are places for both, with a regularity to more traditional, individual classes."

Jennifer Sweet agrees that her individual classes tend to be more traditional also, but adds, "that's usually because of the topic, not because I'm teaching alone." Others nod, but also acknowledge that they usually think of "integrated" and "teaming" as interchangeable terms.

At Forsyth, teams tend to shift throughout the year as courses change with the cycles. While they recognize the stability gained from having more constant teams—which Conelli urges—teachers also like the variety of working with new colleagues, which they believe promotes their own professional growth.

Most of the integrated classes at Forsyth operate a substantial part of the time with all students and staff working in the same room. At a minimum, most classes meet together at the start or end of the period, but split into groups to do project work.

"In the course I'm teaching now, I'm pushing for people working in one room together," say Sarah Blos. "That doesn't get the numbers down, but it does change things. More than one adult in the same room makes it more possible to look at different things. One of us can watch the movement of the course and content, another the mood of the day, while a third can work with individual kids. Our goal is to have it be as fluid as possible in the room."

■ **University Heights High School**. University Heights, located at the Bronx Community College in New York City, was created in 1986 as a "middle college," a school where students attend high school but also benefit from a college environment and the opportunity to take courses at the college. University Heights enrolls 165 students.

From the beginning, interdisciplinary, thematic seminar courses have been central to teaching and learning at the school. University Heights has a weekly schedule similar to Forsyth Street, but with more time built in for family group meetings (Figure 3).

At University Heights, teachers join together to teach a specific course; while some teams remain constant over a year's time, most change membership as new courses begin each semester. Teachers plan the course together and arrive at one grade for each student; credit is split among two or more academic areas.

Suzanne Valenza, Brad Stam, and Augusto Andres teach a course enti-

Figure 3
University Heights High School Schedule*

	Mon	Tue	Wed	Thu	Fri
8:15	Morning Staff Meeting				
8:40	Family Group Meeting				
9:00	Seminar: all staff working on integrated teams				
11:00	Family Group Meeting				
12:00	Lunch				
1:00	E	D	E	E	D
2:00	D	F	D	F	F

Seminar section detail:

	# tchrs	credit areas	planning
Team 1:	3	Eng, sci, h/pe	F
Team 2:	3	Eng, ss, (opt'n'l econ)	F
Team 3:	3,4	Eng, ss, art	D
Team 4:	4	Eng, ss, sci, h/pe	D
Team 5:	2	Eng, art, pe	D
Team 6:	7	Eng, ss, math	E
Team 7:	3	Eng, psy, college prep	E

Teamed staff have common planning time. Teachers may offer two separate courses in their other two teaching slots, or one course which meets in two of the slots. Offering one course results in a lower overall student load.

---

*University Heights also identifies its periods, or "slots," by letters.

tled "We the People." Marsha Lyles, the school's art teacher, spends two class meetings a week with the course and participates in the planning to help infuse art into the curriculum. The course, developed cooperatively with the Social History Project at City University of New York, has an enrollment of about 50 students who earn English, social studies, and art credit.

The Social History Project was designed as a "people's history" and traces American history through four themes: slavery, immigration, industrialization, and unions. The Project provides a videotape and some supporting material on each of the themes, but the bulk of the course development rests with the teachers in each of the four New York City schools participating in the project.

The course was designed originally as an interdisciplinary course in American history and English composition for community colleges; the University Heights staff has added a significant art component.

During one particular class, which meets two hours a day, Lyles conducted the first hour, leading students through a series of sketching and writing exercises, discussions, and a brief lecture—all part of an introduction to the concept of abstract art—while Valenza and Andres assisted from the sidelines, once serving as an example for Lyles. Lyles then introduced a video on dadaism to further focus the lesson. For the final 20 minutes, students split into three groups to discuss the video. Each group met in a separate room with a teacher to lead the discussion.

Valenza, the team's coordinator, talks about the course: "Brad, Marsha, and I have taught the course before. This time through, the course is genuinely integrated, not subject-oriented. I have a particular focus on writing, while Brad's focus tends to be the social context of events, but we all take responsibility for the overall design and conduct of the course," she explains, noting that ". . . we also play off each person's obsessions. One of us pushes for role plays, another for reflection, a third for writing. The result is we have a reasonable balance without a lot of conflict."

She describes this week's activities to illustrate the mix of large and small group activities. "The class met in three groups on Monday to do a writing exercise as an introduction to a unit on immigration. On Tuesday, Brad and I went into some depth with the whole group on immigration. Wednesday, we worked in three groups doing a jigsaw exercise (a cooperative learning technique) in preparation for Friday's class.

"Today's class was a whole group session to introduce an art concept as preparation for a group project incorporating abstract art into the study of immigration. Tomorrow, we'll see a video in one group, then have extended discussions in three groups. The week is unusual in that we are together so much in one group, but you get an idea of the movement back and forth." Her description also reveals a measure of complexity involved when a course is project-based and each project extends over several weeks.

The discussion shifts briefly to that day's class. "Neither Augusto, Brad, nor I felt that we had the expertise we needed to introduce the concept of abstraction, so we relied on Marsha as the expert. We don't do that often, though. Typically, the one of us who knows the most about a particular thing coaches the others during our planning time."

Observations and Issues

■ **The crucial role of principals**. The preceding descriptions focused on the general structure of the schools and on the experience of teachers as they work on integrated teams. Yet, in each school, the principal (and, in the case of Forsyth Street, the coordinator) has played a key role in the development of integrated teaching.

Each has helped to formulate a shared vision of integrated teaching with his or her staff and has continued to hold that vision before the staff as a desired goal. Each has worked to make that goal a reality in a number of ways:

- By securing funding for summer work for staff members interested in integrated teaching
- By making interest in integrated teaching a criterion for selecting new staff
- By building, with staff assistance, a schedule that supports integrated teaching
- By respecting the difference in readiness among staff
- By providing options for staff members who are more or less prepared than others (in each school, some teachers have worked on teams for a number of years, while others are just beginning, and each principal continues to provide options for staff who prefer or want a mix of team-work and individual teaching).

Perhaps most important, each principal relied on teacher judgment about how best to promote and support integrated teaching. Even when shared decision-making has not been a priority in the school, the willingness and ability of the principal to listen carefully to staff analysis and suggestions—and dissent—has been crucial, not only in building trust, but in leading to better decisions about the next best step to take.

At the same time, the trust that has been built has allowed each principal to push hard for his or her own beliefs without the principal-teacher alien-ation that often results when trust is limited.

■ **The need for time**. When asked what was most difficult about integrated teaching, the unanimous response at each school was "finding time to plan together." At each school, teams have common planning time built into their work day, but it is often insufficient, both for the ongoing routines developed when teachers collaborate and for the more intense periods that arise throughout the course.

Forsyth teachers note that they spend more time planning at the beginning of a course and then again near the end, when the focus is on student evaluation. Bruce Shotland at Thayer estimates that his team spent more than 100 hours together during the summer working on the overall organization of their course and the first unit, which lasted for the first nine weeks; for the rest of the year, they will need to generate their material as they go.

They, as does the University Heights team, meet regularly after school or in the evening.

■ **The evolving nature of integrated teaching**. The term "integrated" varies from school to school. The meaning flows both from the teaching arrangements they have constructed at the schools and from the teachers' prior experiences.

At Thayer, for example, integration derives primarily from the overall coherence of the curriculum developed and offered by the team. But at Forsyth, Conelli believes that integrated teaching "involves rethinking how you perceive knowledge, how you talk about it, and how you make it available to students."

The Thayer version of integrated teaching represents a type of collaboration that Pat Wasley, a senior researcher on the Coalition central staff, describes as "division of labor." Each teacher retains subject-specific responsibility, but collaborates to achieve coherence. The integration stems from the fact that teachers plan together so they can help students make the connections as they move from one discipline to the next.

The Thayer team, in its first year together, is beginning to stretch this version by using common material, data, and information across their classes rather than merely pointing out connections.

For the teams at Forsyth and University Heights, "integrated teaching" has a broader meaning. In their approach, knowledge is not compartmentalized, but emerges from broad topics or issues. While teachers draw on their specific discipline to design the course and help students understand the topic, instruction is not based on the "demands" of those disciplines in the conventional sense that teachers and curriculum developers have used that word for the past half century. Each teacher, with occasional exceptions, takes responsibility for all parts of the course content.

■ **Attention to students**. At each of the schools, it is difficult for team teachers to talk together for more than a couple minutes without mentioning a specific student. Teachers know the same students, are often in the same room working with them together at the same time, and have a more intense shared interest in their learning than is typical in most schools.

In each of these schools, very specific, detailed discussions of students are a central part of teachers' conversations during their time together. Indeed, it is one of the constraints on their time. It also gives added focus and value. In many ways, it is the teaching equivalent of the countless hours coaches spend together talking about their players as opposed to their plays; the issue is learners' skills and knowledge and what each learner needs to experience in order to improve.

■ **Complexities of working together**. Teachers who work on integrated teams spend long hours together and frequently develop strong bonds. The bonds reveal themselves in the easy camaraderie visible among team members who have worked together for any length of time, and in the trust they place in one another as they rely on each other's planning, organizational skills, or judgment about how a course needs to proceed, or what approach might be best with a particular student.

At the same time, teachers acknowledge the difficulties. "Coming to a base-line agreement is hardest," notes Sarah Blos of Forsyth. "So much of what you do in class is intuitive—a shared vision is what you want, but it takes time." Her colleague, Alice Braziller, notes that "sometimes we mesh really well, other times we have real differences. Usually, it depends on how hard you want to work."

But even with patience, the ability to cooperate and compromise—particular skills the Forsyth staff believes are needed on a team—differences aren't always resolved. Time plays a role here as well, since both building trust and resolving conflicts are often processes of growth between and among individuals.

In the end, however, teachers feel the complexities of working together also lead to important benefits they are denied when working in isolation, not least of which is that students have better learning experiences. They talk about the exhilaration of working together to pull off something new and difficult.

The nature of their conversations tends to be different as well. For integrated teaching to succeed, teachers need to rethink curriculum, pedagogy, and assessment in fundamental ways—an opportunity rarely afforded them in other circumstances. As a result, their talk is more "intellectual"—sometimes more abstract, more informed by reflection.

Teachers say these conversations were rare in their more traditional practices, and they value the growth they produce. Conversations are at the same time more concrete, in that team members share the same students and responsibility for shaping the nature and quality of ideas, experiences, and relationships provided those students.

Most important, though, they recognize the way their colleagues support them in their efforts to change their teaching practice. When asked what was easy about integrated teaching, the Thayer group responded: "Nothing really, is easy for us, but we know we're on the right track. The support we get from each other for working with kids is great, and we're learning what each kid is doing . . . we have more awareness about the whole kid, and that helps us with our work."

Endnotes

1. The findings of A Study of High Schools are reported in three books: *Horace's Compromise*, by Theodore Sizer; *The Last Little Citadel*, by Robert Hampel; and *The Shopping Mall High School*, by Arthur Powell, Eleanor Farrar, and David K. Cohen. All are published by Houghton Mifflin.

2. While integrated teaching sometimes raises questions about how much credit to award a particular discipline, students earn the same amount of total credit for the class time involved. Integrated teaching, then, is not a way to reduce staffing by giving "double" credit for a course. To our knowledge, no Essential schools have reduced their staff size by moving to integrated teaching. An advantage to integrated teaching is that several schools have managed to lower the total number of students with whom teachers work, making personalization more possible.

Nine Common Principles
Coalition of Essential Schools

1. The school should focus on helping adolescents learn to use their minds well. Schools should not attempt to be "comprehensive" if such a claim is made at the expense of the school's central intellectual purpose.
2. The school's goals should be simple: that each student master a limited number of essential skills and areas of knowledge. While these skills and areas will, to varying degrees, reflect the traditional academic disciplines, the program's design should be shaped by the intellectual and imaginative powers and competencies that students need, rather than necessarily by "subjects" as conventionally defined.

The aphorism "Less is more" should dominate: curricular decisions should be guided by the aim of thorough student mastery and achievement rather than by an effort merely to cover content.

3. The school's goals should apply to all students, while the means to these goals will vary as those students themselves vary. School practice should be tailor-made to meet the needs of every group or class of adolescents.

4. Teaching and learning should be personalized to the maximum feasible extent. Efforts should be directed toward a goal that no teacher have direct responsibility for more than 80 students. To capitalize on this personalization, decisions about the details of the course of study, the use of students' and teachers' time, and the choice of teaching materials and specific pedagogies must be unreservedly placed in the hands of the principal and staff.

5. The governing practical metaphor of the school should be student-as-worker, rather than the more familiar metaphor of teacher-as-deliverer-of-instructional-services. Accordingly, a prominent pedagogy will be coaching, to provoke students to learn how to learn and thus to teach themselves.

6. Students entering secondary school studies are those who can show competence in language and elementary mathematics. Students of traditional high school age but not yet at appropriate levels of competence to enter secondary school studies will be provided intensive remedial work to assist them quickly to meet these standards. The diploma should be awarded upon a successful final demonstration of mastery for graduation—an "Exhibition." This Exhibition by the student of his or her grasp of the central skills and knowledge of the school's program may be jointly administered by the faculty and by higher authorities. As the diploma is awarded when earned, the school's program proceeds with no strict age grading and with no system of "credits earned" by "time spent" in class. The emphasis is on the students' demonstration that they can do important things.

7. The tone of the school should explicitly and self-consciously stress values of unanxious expectation ("I won't threaten you but I expect much of you"), of trust (until abused), and of decency (the values of fairness, generosity, and tolerance). Incentives appropriate to the school's particular students and teachers should be emphasized, and parents should be treated as essential collaborators.

8. The principal and teachers should perceive themselves as generalists first (teachers and scholars in general education) and specialists sec-

ond (expert in but one particular discipline). Staff should expect multiple obligations (teacher-counselor-manager) and a sense of commitment to the entire school.

9. Ultimate administrative and budget targets should include, in addition to total student loads per teacher of 80 or fewer pupils, substantial time for collective planning by teachers, competitive salaries for staff, and an ultimate per pupil cost not to exceed that at traditional schools by more than 10 percent. To accomplish this, administrative plans may have to show the phased reduction or elimination of some services now provided students in many traditional comprehensive secondary schools.

Chapter 4

Interdisciplinary Teaming at the High School

Dustin A. Peters

Interdisciplinary team teaching at the high school level represents a concept whose time has come, and gone, and now has returned again. The NASSP Model Schools initiatives of the late 1960s and early 1970s provided the background and foundation for the work; the present restructuring movement, and in particular that of the Coalition of Essential Schools/RE:Learning, represents a driving force for its return.

Why Interdisciplinary Teams?

The advantages of teaming in the middle school are obvious. But this attitude changes as one enters the doors of most high schools. At that level it's often a matter of "turf control."

The driving force for curriculum and instruction in the classroom is the subject area department, usually under direct control of the department chairperson. The principal in too many high schools has delegated his or her curricular/instructional functions to the departmental level, or it has been taken over from the district by the curriculum coordinator or assistant superintendent for curriculum. The principal schedules at the direction of another informed group, and there is little chance for change or substantive improvement.

Before the implementation of an interdisciplinary teaching team concept, the following conditions must exist at the building level:

1. The principal must be in charge of scheduling, curriculum development, and the instructional process
2. Elective subjects must be reduced in favor of a core of common studies at each grade level

3. Time for dialog and planning of interdisciplinary units of study must be available to teachers.

At Elizabethtown Area High School the first two conditions have always been in place. The third came about with the school's involvement in the Coalition of Essential Schools in the mid-1980s.

As a result of our involvement with the Coalition, the professional staff redirected its attention toward the teaming process. It represented a natural direction for us because it involved teachers in leadership, decision making, and empowerment.

Elizabethtown changed its structure to an interdisciplinary teaching team: a four-teacher team (English, math, science, and social studies) with a common grouping of students. The members of the team are scheduled for two classes in the morning and two classes in the afternoon with three common planning periods in a seven-period schedule. During the three non-classroom periods, team teachers have time for tutorial work, planning, and team meetings. They have no other types of supervision assignments as a part of their school day.

Getting Started

Since 1984, Elizabethtown Area High School has slowly considered and implemented a variety of changes under the broad umbrella of its involvement in the Coalition of Essential Schools. Generally, talking about change is much easier than implementing it.

While it is important to develop and maintain "the conversation," as Theodore Sizer says, when the time arrives to implement the change, a principal needs a solid group of faculty members to help show the "hows" and "whys" of the changes being proposed. It is definitely a "risk-taking" venture. Restructuring is something many schools talk about, less consider, and few do.

As Elizabethtown continued its quest for change, the faculty and staff considered "structure" before "process." They were interested in gradual change, but also in lasting change that would make a difference. Changing structure is significant. If one is able to get a structure in place (interdisciplinary teaching teams), the process usually follows as a natural progression.

Another important factor is determining the target population. Many schools implement "a school-within-a-school" concept focusing on a core of students. A better approach, however, involves expanding that concept to include everyone in the school. Elizabethtown started with three teaching teams—at grades 9, 10, and 11—because the vision was an interdisciplinary teaching team model for the entire school.

Regardless of how one begins interdisciplinary teaming, a natural concomitant in the early stages is the development of a "we-they" attitude. At Elizabethtown, where all the team members were volunteers, there were still problems. The teacher volunteers appeared to have special arrangements, no extra duties, and more planning time.

As we plan for our third year of teaming, the volunteer approach continues. It appears to be working, but some resentment still occurs. Communication plays a major role in helping to address and overcome some of the problems. It's important to use anyone and everyone in this effort.

Presentations at faculty meetings, small group meetings, and the sharing of written documents all represent ways to overcome the "we-they" attitude. Moreover, it requires a continuous effort to share clearly the intended focus and direction to all teachers so everyone can determine his or her role.

One interesting idea being pursued at Elizabethtown is the spring "Annual Interdisciplinary Team Invitational," a meeting where present and potential team members get together to discuss teaming. A major part of the meeting is the social interaction that provides teachers an opportunity to know each other better. As new teams are considered, it is important to learn who can work together and with whom.

The principal serves as a "broker," answering questions, suggesting team makeup, and reviewing possibile combinations. In the end, however, it remains an individual and a team decision as to who joins a team or who comprises a new team organization.

The process in itself is one of "restructuring" at the professional level. Some teams' needs may have to wait for the hiring process to be completed. In this case team members have a role in the decision as to the best person to fit the needs of the team and the teaching assignment.

Scheduling

A commitment of time and money is required to make interdisciplinary teaming work. Team members must understand the extent of the time required to make interdisciplinary teaming successful, and budget administrators must understand the need to fund additional planning opportunities.

Elizabethtown expects that all members of a team will spend a minimum of two summer inservice day meetings to plan interdisciplinary units. Incoming team members agree that 2 units will be developed each year, thus making it possible to develop 10 units in five years. Over time, the curriculum changes substantially, resulting in integrated subject matter and a more personal instructional process.

During the first two years of operation, 1989-1991, team members slowly developed guidelines necessary to make teaming work. During the first year, we actually had four teams, but one of them did not have a common planning period. They never met, except on their own time, and eventually the team disbanded.

That same year, all teams had mixed groups with limited students in common. Team teachers taught five classes in traditional blocks of time that virtually eliminated any large group opportunities. Given this background, one can readily understand why our initial attempts at teaming did not yield the results we hoped. They had nowhere to go to see how it was done.

Fortunately, we learned as we went, making adjustments on the run and developing better plans for the following year.

In the second year team teachers were scheduled for four periods of teaching, two in the morning and two in the afternoon. This arrangement gave them almost 100 minutes to work with students in a traditional classroom setting or to bring them together for large group presentations.

Students were hand-scheduled for the three teams so the same students could be assigned to the same team. The results were impressive. The teams were empowered to work with their students in more personalized ways.

For the coming year, Elizabethtown hopes to further improve its scheduling process and to implement a model that could be shared with interested schools. An example of this for ninth grade (the easiest one) is listed in Figure 1.

Figure 1

Team A	Courses Common to A or B	Team B
English	PE/Health	English
Math	Music	Math
Science	Business	Science
Social Studies	Art	Social Studies
	Other Electives	
French I/II		Spanish I/II
German I/II		Home Economics
Agriculture		Industrial Arts

This represents a move to a type of scheduling whereby elective courses are either part of side A or side B, or common to both sides. Of course, the ninth grade schedule is the easiest to develop. As one advances to grades 10, 11, and 12, the process is more complex. The development of a common core of studies for all students at each grade level helps to reduce the complexity.

Eventually, this type of scheduling will be included as a part of the course selection process. It will enable elective teachers to form linkages with specific teaching teams; initially, for interaction about students, but later for developing and teaching interdisciplinary units with the elective as a focus for the unit.

Departments and Teams

The subject area department is one of the many structures that remain in all schools. Areas of the building are often grouped around departments. Departmental members address specific issues including curriculum budget and staffing.

The interdisciplinary teaching team complements departmentalization and provides a balance. It gradually moves the focus from a single subject to a bigger picture, the total learning environment and the interrelatedness of subject matter.

Ultimately, the departmental barriers are broken down, and an enhanced decision-making role for team members evolves. Interdisciplinary teaching becomes the "instructional process" in the school's efforts to improve the learning environment. Subject area departments still remain as a "product control" element raising questions about content, scope, and sequence. But in the end, the teams will change the instructional process to include the "student-as-worker and the teacher-as-coach."

The potential for teaming in terms of curriculum and instruction speaks for itself. Elizabethtown Area High School in a short time has created exciting units around the daily newspaper, environmental issues, and community concerns. We have also introduced units on "when am I ever going to use this"—linking careers to the subjects and "thinking about thinking"—reviewing problem solving and relating it to the various subject areas as a group.

An equally important change, and a direct result of teaming, is an emphasis on personalization. Each team member functions as an adviser to the common students. They get to know students better, talk about them and their problems much more, and address concerns, all in a team format.

This process results in more attention being focused to the personal and academic needs of individual students.

But, personalization is not just for students. Teaming creates a special kind of professional support for teachers that sometimes becomes a personal one as well. The teaming concept, with adequate time for planning and meeting students, results in new and improved roles for teachers. Gone are the lunchtime monitoring assignments and hall duty. In its place are responsibilities that directly support the learning process and the students on the team.

During the 1990-91 school year, the teaching team staff at Elizabethtown drafted a *Job Description* for the non-classroom portion of their teaching responsibilities. The following paragraph presents a summary of those responsibilities:

> The nonclassroom assignment for the Coalition of Essential Schools' staff plays a significant role in the personal, collegial, and academic needs of both students and professional staff. It serves to provide a fresh personal opportunity to meet students one-on-one or in small group situations. It also allows teachers to meet in a vital "team meeting" format as necessary. The collegial aspect provides time for team interaction and contacts with other professionals: guidance, support staff, administration, other teaching teams, elective teachers, and visitors/observers. Lastly, and equally important, is the increased instructional planning time available to the team members.

Team members spend a lot of time in personal acquaintance interviews/ conferences, reviewing personal files of students, reading student journals, serving as advisers, pursuing tutorial efforts, coordinating individual/team discipline issues, and monitoring student management issues such as attendance and scheduling.

A Restructuring Attitude

The principal and key staff members must communicate the advantages of interdisciplinary teaming to the entire faculty. This can be accomplished in many ways. The following have worked at Elizabethtown Area High School:

- A *Professional Inservice Reading Project* in which the entire staff reads a book, such as *Horace's Compromise* by Theodore Sizer, discussing its content and implication for the school.

- *Ideal/Reality Exercises* in which teachers and/or students compare the ideal teaching or learning situation with the real one.
- *Shadow Studies* in which staff members follow a student for a full day of the schedule.
- *School Visitations* in which staff members visit several schools involved in restructuring activities.

All of these exercises are designed to get the professional staff thinking about improvements for the school program. Change is a slow process with changing roles and responsibilities for the principal and the teachers. The process can be an exciting one filled with exhilarating moments of growth, often preceded by moments of frustration. But, if the conversation continues, all of the participants will gain from the experience, and the ultimate benefit will be enhanced learning opportunities for the students and teachers in your building.

Chapter 5

The Micro-Society School

Donald P. Hayes, Sue Ellen Hogan, Thomas F. Malone

Superintendent of Schools Patrick J. Mogan viewed the city of Lowell, Mass., as an educative city whose rich cultural and industrial heritage could be explored by students and adults alike.

In his book, *The Micro-Society School: A Real World in Miniature*, George Richmond describes his early attempts at building a miniature society in his New York City classroom that included a currency, businesses, newspapers, courts, and a government.

The visions of the "city as a classroom" and a school classroom as a "miniature society" were the foundation of the Clement G. McDonough City Magnet School, which opened in Lowell in September 1981.

Today, the McDonough City Magnet School is located in the downtown center of Lowell, a working class city of more than 100,000 people which continues its immigrant tradition with Hispanics and Southeast Asians as the major groups. The school's 335 students are a demographic mix of 55 percent majority and 45 percent minority students with 60 percent within the lower socioeconomic guidelines of the federal lunch program.

This school was one of two citywide magnet schools opened to provide a vehicle for voluntary desegregation and an alternative educational program for parents, students, and teachers.

In 1987 a specially renovated building that had been designed for the micro-society was opened. Special areas for such activities as the court, the legislature, the marketplace, banks, and newspapers were built for the active involvement of students in creating their own miniature world.

The micro-society curriculum at the City Magnet School provides students with the opportunity, within the school building, to develop and conduct their own micro-society, based on free-market and democratic principles. In the micro-society, students are not "immature" citizens of a larger society, but mature citizens of their own society.

In this environment, students recognize that basic skills are necessary to function in their society. Students use reading and writing skills as they publish a variety of newspapers, magazines, and books. Math skills are utilized as students develop and operate businesses and banks. Social studies skills come alive as students learn the value of citizenship while they conduct their own legislative, executive, and judicial institutions within their own government. Science and high tech become meaningful to students as they operate their own word/data processing businesses or publish their science research papers.

The school day is composed of the City Magnet "academy" and the micro-society activities. In the "academy" classes, students prepare for placement exams in the four "curriculum strands"—publishing, economy, citizenship/government, and science/high technology. They choose occupations based on their performance on the placement exams and teacher informal assessment. The higher the score a student earns on an exam, the more responsible the position he or she can choose. Students who take the accounting exams, for example, are eligible for jobs as managers, assistant managers, loan managers, tellers, and assistant tellers in the micro-society banks. They can also be owners or employees in a marketplace business.

Students are eligible for promotion based on ongoing evaluation of their job performance by the teacher and student supervisor. The wages for these jobs are paid in "Mogans," the school currency. Every student *must* participate in each of the four micro-society strands during his or her tenure at the City Magnet School.

The micro-society is a developmental K-8 curriculum. Students in the "primary" cluster (K-3), and the "intermediate" cluster (4-6), are expected to master skills appropriate to their level of educational development. Students in the "senior" cluster (7-8) master more sophisticated skills.

The 120 seventh and eighth grade students at the City Magnet are taught by a team of four teachers; students in each grade are grouped heterogeneously.

Each of the four classroom teachers in a cluster specializes in teaching one of the four curriculum strands—publishing, economy, citizenship/government and science/high tech. This specialization, however, does not mean they work in isolation; the teachers work as a team responsible for the development of the "whole" child. The cluster teachers work closely to plan and schedule "academy" classes. Some of this cluster planning has evolved into developing various interdisciplinary units and more cooperative learning groups.

During preparation periods and bi-monthly curriculum development workshops, the cluster teachers also communicate with their colleagues in the other clusters. This is particularly useful in facilitating micro-society activity planning. The teachers are constantly working to develop new "academy" lessons that will make connections between the basic skills and the experience of the students in the micro-society activities.

In the publishing "academy" classes, students are taught the writing, editing, and layout skills that are later applied to produce newspapers, magazines, and books in a micro-society publishing activity. In the process, spelling, grammar, and other language arts skills are also taught in a publishing context. Reading skills are taught through both newspapers and literature-based tradebooks. Research skills are taught in conjunction with citizenship and science research assignments. Students are encouraged in the computer lab to apply the Macintosh and Apple IIGs word processing skills to produce these interdisciplinary assignments.

In the economy "academy" classes, students are taught basic math and accounting skills, as well as economic principles. Through the use of micro-society-based case studies, students learn how to solve computation and word problems while using sales/expense ledgers and profit/loss statements. These skills are later useful to the students as they operate a business in the micro-society marketplace. Lessons about interest and banking also take on new meaning to the students, when they know that they will later apply these skills in the context of operating the two micro-society banks.

The entire micro-society economy offers the teachers a rich opportunity to develop lessons on such economic principles as deficit, inflation, and supply/demand. Economy class skills are also applied across the curriculum strands, as evidenced by students operating a publishing business or the government's IRS and Treasury Departments.

In citizenship/government "academy" classes, students learn the meaning of being a citizen of the world, country, city, and micro-society. As citizens of the micro-society, they learn about the legislative, executive, and judicial branches of their government in the student-written "City Magnet School Constitution." They learn the "school laws" that have been passed during the years by the 28-member student legislature and are introduced to court procedure.

Citizens must know this material well, especially if they want to run for office or become government workers, court officers, lawyers, or judges. The students begin to develop a sophisticated, first-hand understanding of the workings of government, as they later work at these micro-society activity jobs.

This understanding can be used as an "experience base" from which students are able to compare the micro-society government with city, state, national, and international governments. This experience base can also be applied later to their understanding of the issues that face governments.

For example, the student legislature must develop a budget for the government. Just like their adult counterparts, the students must deal with the issues of fair wages, government services, constituent needs, taxes, government deficits, and even welfare for bankrupt students. Similarly, student judges, lawyers, and court officers, just like their adult counterparts, must be cognizant of defendent's and plaintiff's civil rights.

These experiences, just like other micro-society experiences, can be used by the teacher as grist for further lessons in the "academy" setting, as the students study world and U.S. history. The experiences that the students bring with them from the micro-society, particularly in the areas of economics and government, help them develop a better understanding of the issues surrounding events such as the Great Depression, or the Persian Gulf crisis.

In the science/high tech strand, the newest of the four curriculum strands, basic skills are also taught. In the science/high tech "academy" class, the time is divided between learning earth or life science and learning about computers. In the science lab the emphasis is on students learning how to perform, as well as document, science experiments. These experiments can later be shared with younger students.

Students are also expected to do science research assignments. These assignments are later published as books or articles that can be shared with younger students and/or sold to the school library.

In the computer lab, students are given the opportunity to develop their word and data processing skills. Later, students market these skills as a service that can be provided to the various governmental departments, banks, businesses, or individual students.

Case in Point

As noted earlier, the cluster teachers have made a particular effort to develop interdisciplinary units that call on students to apply their computer skills in combination with their other skills. In the computer lab, the teacher will not only work with the students on their computer skills, but will also show him or her how to access additional information for this assignment through use of the modem.

Application of micro-society skills and experiences in an interdisciplinary context cannot always be planned by the teachers. They must also be ready to respond to unanticipated events stimulated by the micro-society and/or by the macro-society.

One example of an unanticipated event that led to the use of micro-society skills in an interdisciplinary context occurred in the spring of 1990. The vice president of the student body initiated a motion in the legislature to place a soft drink machine in or near the school cafeteria. In the course of the debate the grade 2-8 legislators discussed nutritional issues they learned in science. A juice machine was proposed as a compromise and a legislative subcommittee appointed.

This subcommittee was responsible for conducting a market survey, addressing staff concerns, negotiating a location, evaluating vendor "deals," recommending staffing, establishing usage guidelines, recycling, establishing a job description, and allocating profits. Two employees were responsible for ordering, restocking, record keeping, bill paying, and making bank deposits during the micro-society activity period.

Shortly after the machine was in place, a governmental agency review team ruled that the juice machine was in violation of the federal lunch program regulation. The review team required that juice sales cease. This ruling also affected other student groups, who were running popcorn and bake sales.

Students in the legislature demanded, "How can they take our machine away? WE passed a law to have it, and WE did all the work to put it in and run it. That is OUR machine, not theirs!" All appeared lost to the students. But then a seventh and eighth grade teacher challenged them with, "What do you want to do about this? Be angry or take some action?" The classes discussed what actions they could take and decided to write individually to their congressman about the situation.

Within a few days the congressman's office called the principal for more information on the issue. Shortly thereafter, the congressman's office responded with a policy clarification from the U.S. Department of Agriculture. The ruling was that nutritious juice drinks and baked goods were appropriate to be sold during lunch periods.

This experience made it clear to the students that the interdisciplinary skills and the attitudes taught as part of the micro-society curriculum have direct application to the macro-society. In addition, they also learned how to effect change within the system and that the democratic system works for citizens who get involved.

A Work in Progress

The McDonough City Magnet School is not a finished product but a "work in progress." Teachers, parents, students, and administrators continually collaborate to improve the school and refine their vision of the micro-society theme. This school community is a vital center of learning and growth. The micro-society curriculum flourishes through the active involvement of all constituencies.

Future goals include:

- Implementing a pilot program in school-based management
- Expanding the micro-society curriculum and activities
- Continuing to explore the city of Lowell as a classroom.

The micro-society curriculum is certainly not an easy curriculum to implement. It can be done, however, as demonstrated recently by the principal and staff at the fledgling Yonkers, N.Y., micro-society school.

The reward cannot only be quantified in test scores, which indicate that students at the McDonough city magnet school test either at or near the top of the Lowell Public Schools, especially in the area of math and critical thinking skills. The reward is not just the nationwide recognition or the 1985 award from the Massachusetts State Department of Education for implementing a quality desegregation program. The rewards of teaching and working in a micro-society school are not always as tangible.

The reward for a principal and his or her staff comes when they see inner-city students and teachers eager to come to school, when they are able to see the eager anticipation on the faces of the students, as they go to their jobs in the micro-society areas for the first time. The reward can also be found as they watch a formerly shy, grade 7 girl not only grow into her role as a lawyer, but defend her client's rights as vigorously as Perry Mason.

To duplicate the micro-society at the McDonough City Magnet School, certain elements must be in place, including:

1. The commitment and support of the superintendent and the central administration.
2. Funding that can be used for staff and curriculum development workshops, micro-society supplies, and a program facilitator who can assist with on-going program development.
3. Strong educational leadership from the principal that provides for shared decision making.
4. The empowerment of the teachers, parents, and students to make decisions that will affect them, and thus contribute to ownership of decisions by all constituents.

5. The commitment of a volunteer teaching staff to make it work.
6. A prevailing attitude that the micro-society is not a finished product, but a "work in progress."

For more than nine years, supplementary Massachusetts Chapter 636 funding has enabled the teachers, the principal, and the program facilitator to continue to work on Mogan's and Richmond's vision. The task of refining the micro-society curriculum continues in bi-monthly curriculum development workshop sessions.

Throughout this process, parent and student input into the decision making has been continued. Through their respective participatory organs—the Parent Teacher Organization Executive Board and the student legislature—parents and students are also able to contribute to the evolving micro-society curriculum.

In addition, the School Improvement Executive Council's monthly meetings have given parents, teachers, students, and administrators a common forum for sharing in a schoolwide decision-making process. The empowerment and ownership that have resulted from this shared decision making have enabled the micro-society curriculum to evolve successfully despite some trying times.

Chapter 6

The Core: Integrated Curriculum and Student Support
A Case Study

Suzanne R. Krumbein, Gerald Krumbein

For some time now, educators have recognized the unique characteristics of adolescents. Physically, they are growing and changing, experiencing hormonal imbalances, and developing secondary sex characteristics. A heightened consciousness of their bodies causes them perpetual consternation, as each child secretly believes that the physical changes he or she is undergoing are unique.

Emotionally, adolescents behave inconsistently, demanding independence but needing security, often overreacting, and having, for all their bluster and "know-it-allness," a surprisingly fragile sense of self-esteem.

Socially, they want desperately to belong to a group. Their focus is shifting from their families to their friends. They continue to need the approval of their parents and teachers but keep that need a secret from everyone, especially their friends. The social aspect of life is very important to middle level students, often occupying, as far as adults are concerned, much too much of their energy and interest. Intellectually, adolescents are curious but prefer active to passive learning experiences. They vary in maturation rate, with some students ready for abstract reasoning and others still needing very concrete experiences. Like all students, adolescents have different learning styles and rates, and students of the same chronological age may be at very different places academically.

The knowledge that adolescents have their own particular characteristics and needs should assist middle school staff members in planning the school's organizational pattern, styles of instructional delivery, and the kinds of experiences it wants for students. Unfortunately, this does not often occur. Many middle schools are still organized like mini-high schools with seven single period classes, no teacher more than once a day, and no adult that the students can call their own or with whom they feel any special kinship or relationship.

The short attention span of young adolescents, plus their eagerness for active learning, make the formal lecture style of teaching rather limiting and ineffective in the middle school. However, instruction that is followed by activity, including having students work individually, in pairs, or in groups, is very satisfying to middle school students. In fact, when faced with a large block of time, students do much better with a variety of shorter activities than with one extended lesson. The wise teacher moves them from one task to another before boredom sets in.

Specifically, students at our middle school are assigned to a core class three periods per day where the content includes reading, English, social studies, and advisory. The core teacher is also responsible for parent conferences. The most important aspect of this core program is the amount of time one group of students has with one teacher. Both the students and the teacher need to spend enough time together to get to know each other well, to pursue subjects that are important but might not be discussed in a single class period, to deal with organization that is a real challenge for many young adolescents, and to integrate the subjects and the skills involved.

They also need to have the time to establish a relationship that will allow the teacher to support and help students through the myriad social and personal problems that are endemic to this age group and which can overshadow and interfere with academic progress.

A Core Program Case Study

The following description illustrates how one core program is structured with these needs in mind.

By 7:50 a.m., students are arriving at school, coming into the room to put their books down, say good morning, check on the plan for the day, and then go out to see who is "doing what with whom."

This is a common mode of operation with my students. They may not necessarily want to spend a great deal of time with the teacher, but need to touch base and make sure they know what's going on. Some want to tell something that happened the previous evening or go over a problem assignment. Regardless of whether the teacher converses with a student for two seconds or two minutes, it is the opportunity to make contact that pleases both and provides the security students need as a foundation for building a positive relationship.

When class starts at 8:20, the structure is more formal. After the Pledge of Allegiance and announcements, we review the morning's agenda and then do whatever housekeeping is necessary. Because the class is fresh, the lesson is conducted with the entire class, followed by an individual or group activity based on the lesson.

For example, the teacher may ask students to get out an essay in progress for review. Perhaps half a dozen students will read their introductory paragraphs aloud. After we have talked about what makes a good first paragraph, students have about 20 minutes for writing, with the teacher circulating first to students who seem to be having difficulty, but then generally checking on student progress. A special point is made to have some kind of contact with each student. At the end of the writing time, several students might be asked to read what they have written before we put the essay away to be finished for homework that night.

As the morning progresses, students are moved through a series of lessons, saving the more active events for later in the period when they might be getting a bit restless. For example, the state of the oral book reports might be discussed. Then the groups will meet at tables, finishing their scripts to turn in at the end of a 20-minute work period. Again, the teacher circulates among groups. The scripts are collected with 10 minutes left in the block.

The next day's vocabulary lesson is reviewed, reminding students of the specific steps they should take by choosing one of the words and actually going through the learning steps with the entire class.

Thus, during this one double period block of 90-100 minutes, the teacher provided four integrated activities:

1. Conducted a writing lesson
2. Reviewed the process of a group project
3. Moved from group to group during work time
4. Assisted the students in starting their vocabulary assignment.

Students are busy and focused with no time for "less productive" or disruptive activity. In addition, during the entire time, the teacher has been circulating and meeting with individual students about a variety of problems and issues, running the gamut from academic to social to emotional. Young adolescents like variety but also need real structure. It is imperative, if they are to be successful, that their teachers provide both. This not only enhances academics, but minimizes discipline problems.

Three or four events are planned for this morning block, so the teacher has time to speak to quite a few students individually. This time is absolutely invaluable. Without it, students would have to come in during lunch or after school, or before or after class, which is always a busy time.

Some students may be embarrassed or unwilling to ask for help but need it, nonetheless, and the teacher can easily speak to them on a regular basis while making the rounds of the room.

By the time December rolls around, the teacher knows the core class very well, having observed their mode of operation and individual learning styles as well as their levels of achievement.

The teacher is able to pursue subjects that would not be possible in a single period class. Adolescents are very interested in what's happening around school. Sometimes a morning announcement is somewhat controversial. This might involve a school dance, litter on the yard, or vandalism to a bathroom. Students might have information about the incident or comments about how it is being handled. They are often eager to talk about the situation.

The teacher may find that they are misinformed, and much can be cleared up by calling the office with a question or asking our student council representative to bring up this subject at the next meeting. In fact, some of the most important lessons students learn are from impromptu discussions. Students know there is more to school and growing up than organized classes.

Of course, extended time also works well when an academic topic is of great interest, and students have the option of pursuing it further. A student may comment about a news item that is of special interest to someone else in the class. This flexibility in using time makes these "departures" from the day's agenda enjoyable because we know we have the time to get back to our planned activities.

An extended period of time with one teacher also gives students the opportunity to acquire good organizational skills—an important area for the core teacher to emphasize. This can be accomplished by writing the week's plan on the board Monday morning, and having everyone copy it onto an assignment sheet.

The students know that once they have filled out their assignment sheet and put it in their binder, they have a record of assignments due, reading that must be done, and materials to bring to class during the week. They know whether or not they will be writing in class, discussing a portion of a novel, taking a test, or listening to speeches. They can plan ahead if they have a busy evening or just check the assignment sheet before they pack their books to go home after school.

In addition to outlining the week's work on the board, the teacher can spend some time on Monday morning talking about what kind of week it is going to be. Is there an important assignment that they must work on right away? How might they best use their time? Should they ask a parent to quiz them on the material for the social studies test?

As students improve their organizational skills, their achievement tends to improve as well, because of the increased focus and the belief that they have more control over their own destiny. Having the time to work on these skills is a real advantage of the core block.

Within the core itself, one of the greatest rewards for the teacher is to be able to integrate skills and subjects that are often taught individually. Very little in the real world is as compartmentalized as the traditional junior or senior high school. Integrating subjects can make them much more relevant and meaningful to students. A writing lesson can focus on literature or social studies. Students' oral skills can be developed by assigning them to give speeches as historical figures.

Not only do students benefit academically from writing and speaking about the social studies material they are learning, but they find it more interesting. In fact, the love of the dramatic moment can be used to great advantage in the middle school. Students enjoy writing skits and performing them. Costumes and props enrich the experience. They find it even more exciting when the skit is videotaped.

Of course, this type of activity is an almost insurmountable challenge for the teacher with a single period. The longer core block makes it possible.

Because core teachers see students for a greater block of time each day, they generally initiate and plan field trips and special events. All sixth graders participate in Greek Week, a week-long celebration of their study of Greece. Each class performs a play they have written and students participate in athletic contests as the Greeks did. They dress as Greeks and have a Greek luncheon.

In seventh grade, the core teachers plan and carry out a Renaissance Faire, a day-long event during which seventh graders dress in Renaissance costumes, run booths, put on plays and other appropriate performances, and eat food typical of the time.

Eighth graders conclude their study of American history by assembling an American history museum which they present for Open House. Each class puts together displays and exhibits on events that took place during a particular period of American history. The following day, eighth graders come to school dressed as people did during the period they studied and participate in a variety of events. They tour the exhibits, attend an assembly where class quilts, speeches, and skits are presented, and then have an all-

American lunch of hamburgers and hot dogs prepared by parents. After lunch, they square dance and then conclude the day with softball games.

Besides special events such as these, core teachers organize field trips to an Egyptian museum, Chinatown in San Francisco, and to the theater. These involve all the students on one grade level. These events, which involve students in activities that require higher order thinking skills, are some of the most significant and memorable experiences they will have in school.

Non-core organizations rarely have these kinds of experiences for students—due not to a lack of teacher interest, energy, or expertise, but to a lack of time in class.

In addition to a three-period language arts/social studies core, the eighth graders have four periods of instruction per day: math, science, physical education, and an elective, such as French, Spanish, art, drama, woodshop, and computers. Our sixth graders participate in an exploratory program, the forerunner of an elective program. They move through a variety of subjects, including foreign language, computers, art, and drama. Seventh graders choose electives just like the eighth graders do.

During the seven-period day, students are grouped heterogeneously in all classes except math, where the current philosophy on grouping is causing the staff to reexamine this last bastion of tracking. It is our firm conviction that all students deserve "equal access" to the most advanced levels of the curriculum offered.

Advisory

An additional aspect of the core program that benefits teachers and students is *advisory*. Our *advisory* takes place once a week during one period taken from the core block and can be taught by the counselor or teacher. The goal of the advisory program is to formally integrate certain relevant but traditionally non-academic topics and skills into the curriculum. These topics include relationships with other people, decision making, goal setting, and adolescents and the law.

Lessons may vary from watching a videotape about juveniles in court, to discussing decisions one might make in certain situations, to planning a 10-year high school reunion. The lessons are planned and specific, and can either be developed by staff or can be purchased "ready-made." Either way, it is important that teachers not be burdened individually with the creation of advisory curriculum.

Advisory time allows both the teacher and the students to focus on subjects that otherwise might only be talked about by students at recess. This allows some adult guidance in an area where it hasn't occurred before in school. It is also a time when students can bring up subjects that interest them and that they often see as important, but which are rarely discussed during class.

Cocurricular activities are planned by the student activities director with assistance from the student council. These generally take place during the lunch hour and include intramurals, dress-up days, and contests. Student can try out for and participate in the talent show or a musical. The school and the recreation department also cooperate to run an after-school sports program.

Announcements about programs and information that students need to participate in these activities is generally given during core. Again, the time is available, and the core teacher is ever aware of how important school activities are in creating spirit in the classroom.

Making a Difference

One of the results of a multi-block core program is an increased sense of student self-esteem. Students know their core teacher has time to get to know them, to help them, and to praise them for what they do. They can see that the school as a whole values their work, whether it is academic, athletic, dramatic, musical, artistic, or organizational. The evidence is there daily, in what people say and what is displayed for everyone to see.

At an awards ceremony at the end of each quarter, many students are rewarded for a job well done. They receive awards from teachers and from the student council for academic achievement, school service, sports, and a positive attitude. The wide variety of awards allows many students to be singled out.

Are there any drawbacks to the kind of core program and the hetero-geneous grouping of middle school students described here? You really have to decide whether or not the benefits of a core program are important enough to make the scheduling concessions that will be necessary. Obviously, whether a school decides on a two period or three period core block, this program has to be scheduled first in order to have at least two periods together. Other subjects will naturally be affected, and some sched-uling flexibility will be lost.

Since the goal of any school is to be successful, the core program is one that many people will embrace when they see what a difference it makes to students. However, teachers moving from a single period schedule to a core block need assistance in learning how to integrate subjects and how to use a longer block of time. These are not things all teachers know how to do, and staff will certainly feel more comfortable making this change if they know they will get district and collegial support as they learn. Perhaps a common planning time for teachers at one grade level is important, at least in the beginning, so that they can get together to plan or to discuss problems.

Another alternative is a restructured week with planning time regularly set aside for teachers to work together. At my school, students go home early every Thursday to give teachers time to meet and develop grade level and curricular expectations and experiences. This has been a real boon to my staff.

Perhaps the bottom line is the needs of students. The school staff must keep in mind adolescents' need for a structured situation in which a caring individual creates a challenging but supportive program. This kind of environment can only be established through a program in which a teacher has sufficient time with students. It is also important to remember that core functions as a stabilizer. It is, in effect, a student's home away from home. In fact, for many students from dysfunctional homes, it could very well be the only stable aspect of their lives.

Given the importance of core, the selection of core teachers deserves at least a mention. The core teacher serves the dual role of teacher/counselor. As a result, the person assigned to teach core should be someone who genuinely likes and understands adolescents but realizes that they need structure and firm guidelines. Since the core teacher is the one who communicates most frequently with parents, he or she should have a good grasp of both adolescent development and the techniques that help adolescents function successfully both at home and at school.

Perhaps more important, the core teacher also needs to have a good sense of humor, a willingness to have fun, and the ability to not take himself or herself too seriously.

Of course, the community has a stake in the way the curriculum is organized in the middle school. Although we would say that most parents support a core block, the one thing that worries them is that their child might be assigned to a less than excellent core teacher. This is a very valid concern and one that is likely to be expressed by parents whose children attend a middle school where certain core teachers are seen as inadequate. This problem needs to be solved by the administration at the school site.

The major question, then, is whether a school that does not have a core program can successfully and effectively meet the needs of sixth, seventh, and eighth graders. Our answer to that is an unequivocal "No!" Middle school students deserve to spend at least a double period per day with a teacher who can play several roles in their lives: teacher, counselor, advocate, and even friend.

Without this relationship, the young adolescent may merely move through school as another name on a class list and pass on to high school as anonymously as he or she entered middle school two or three years earlier.

Chapter 7

Project 2061: Science for All Americans

Andrew Ahlgren

In 1989, after more than three years of work, Project 2061 released *Science for All Americans* (SFAA), a statement about what students should know in the areas of science, mathematics, and technology when they leave high school.

Now, in the second phase of Project 2061, recommendations are being developed regarding how schools can attain the goals of SFAA. Several alternative models for K-12 curriculum will be released in 1993, but that's not the end of the work. A school district that wishes to use one of the curriculum models released in 1993 will probably need to take a year or more to modify the models to fit local conditions and preferences.

The premise of Project 2061 is that a curriculum must be developed by the people who will be using it. The details—the particular materials, settings, and time schedules—will be different for every site and faculty. The teachers in every school will want to adapt, fill in, and flesh out the model in ways suited to their students, community, and environment. In addition, teachers will understand a curriculum—its content and methods—only if they have a hand in crafting it themselves.

Although Phase I produced a single set of goals, a floor that all high school graduates should have attained and retained, it is not the intent in Phase II to develop a single curriculum aimed at those goals. There are many alternative ways to help students learn. We commissioned six different teams to develop six different curriculum models. The teams are located in school districts in Philadelphia, San Francisco, San Diego, San Antonio, the small town of McFarland, Wis., and a consortium of three rural districts in Georgia. Each model is to include K-12 and account for goals in natural and social science, mathematics, and technology.

Each development team comprises approximately 25 educators: elementary, middle, and high school teachers of science, mathematics, social studies, and industrial arts; a principal from each of these levels; and usually a few central administrators. Work is typically done in small groups whose members represent a wide range of backgrounds.

A school or school district adapting a curriculum model must involve teachers from the full range of grade levels. Each level has vital contributions to make to planning the flow of learning.

Learning is seldom a series of mastering pieces. Almost all ideas and skills involve a growing sophistication over time, often without definitive milestones that would signal "mastery." Accordingly, teachers at different grade levels cannot set achievement requirements for one another. Rather, they must cooperate in planning what the flow of increasing sophistication and learning experiences will be like, regardless of the precise grade in which they occur.

Before curriculum planning began, teams were enjoined to think through some entire K-12 paths of understanding for twelfth-grade outcomes stated in SFAA. For example, one outcome under the section titled The Earth specifies an understanding of the cycle in which water falls as rain, evaporates, condenses as clouds, and falls again to the surface—the "water cycle." What prior understandings must be developed by students in order to understand this cycle, and when can they be learned?

Rather than step back a grade or two at a time (e.g., what would students be able to understand of this by eighth grade?), we found it much more productive to jump all the way down to the primary school. We asked, "What ideas could children learn at the beginning of school that would start them toward eventually understanding the water cycle by the twelfth grade?" This obviously also entails thinking about what ideas and skills children bring to school with them.

The basic knowledge that we identified for primary children was that water tends to disappear when left lying around, and that water tends to appear on the outside of cold glasses. Over several years, the project will work toward connecting these two phenomena by introducing the idea of water becoming an invisible vapor. Eventually ideas of small, invisible particles will be introduced, leading to development of more formal ideas about the molecular nature of matter. Also presented along the way will be the notion that everything has to come from somewhere and go somewhere. Much later, this concept will be understood formally as the conservation of matter.

In imagining steps in the gradual development of understanding, teams had to rely chiefly on their experience and intuition. Sometimes educational research helped them. In addition, the reverse of the typical top-down prescription may come into play: elementary teachers will tell secondary teachers how far elementary school students take a concept and what job will therefore remain for secondary school. But the more likely result of this kind of reflection on children's understanding is a consensus by teachers at all levels of what understanding of an idea means and how it is likely to grow.

Some of the teams have been reluctant to assign levels of understanding to particular grade levels. They suggest that the level of sophistication of particular students in particular topics is important, and that any one student making a certain step in understanding may have only a slight relationship to grade level. The curriculum therefore has to include the means of assessing what the understanding of each student is and the means of helping that student move ahead.

The initial work of the six teams on curriculum models was completed in June 1991. Thereafter, five members of each team will, together with central Project 2061 staff, form an extended Editorial Board to refine the models over the next year. During the latter half of 1992, the final drafts of set of models will be reviewed and revised on the basis of feedback from reviewers for release in mid-1993.

But new curriculum models are not likely to survive in today's school systems unless many other changes occur as well. As the models are being refined, other groups of experts will be constructing "blueprints" for school-system changes that will be necessary to enable the survival of those models.

The blueprints will include teacher education, testing, materials and technology, school organization, parents and communities, curriculum connections (to other parts of the curriculum), higher education connections, equity, policy, and educational research. The blueprints also will be released in 1993.

In addition to the models and blueprints, the 1993 publications will include a guide to practical steps for implementing the changes in real school districts. To tie all this together for the many different audiences, separate special-audience reports will pull from all the publications the most relevant ideas for teachers, for principals, for school-board members, for business and industry, and so on.

If adoption requires two years of in-school work by teachers to prepare for classroom implementation, the first wave of adoptions will not actually reach classrooms until 1995. Some especially eager and bold school districts may begin to use draft materials as early as 1991 and be able to move into classrooms in 1993.

Although this pace must seem slow to a profession that has become accustomed to various quick fixes, we believe that the deliberate pace is absolutely necessary to producing a solid, viable, and lasting change in curriculum and instruction. Will the science and technology content get stale during the process? We think not, for we have focused on the fundamental and cross-cutting ideas that will continue to be a basis for further understanding well into the next century.

References

American Association for the Advancement of Science: A Project 2061 Report on Literacy Goals in Science, Mathematics, and Technology. *Science For All Americans*. Washington, D.C., 1989.

Bar, Varda. "Children's Views About the Water Cycle." *Science Education* 4(1989): 481-500.

Stavy, Ruth. "Children's Conception of Changes in the State of Matter: From Liquid (or Solid) to Gas." *Journal of Research in Science Teaching* 3(1990): 247-66.

Chapter 8

Environmental Education: An Opportunity for Interdisciplinary and Multidisciplinary Curriculum Planning

John Ramsey

The task of recasting American K-12 curricula to include an environmental dimension poses not only significant challenges, but also untapped potential, particularly with respect to opportunities for interdisciplinary arrangements.

To understand this potential we must first examine the current status of environmental education (EE) in K-12 curricular programs. The last national curricular study of environmental education, conducted by Childress in 1978, suggests that environmental education, if it exists at all, is loosely implemented and has little sense of direction. Fewer than 40 percent of those surveyed in the Childress study of 301 environmental education programs considered the following to be "primary" objectives:

- Synthesizing various alternative solutions to environmental problems into a comprehensive plan
- Analyzing the role of contributing factors (technology, legislation, etc.) to the causes of environmental problems
- Evaluating how varying value systems modify and shape the environment
- Developing proficiency to environmental data collection.

Childress concluded that most environmental programs emphasized imparting knowledge of the environment and an appreciation of its resources rather than helping students develop the knowledge and skills to solve environmental problems. Most programs do not embrace or focus on a clearly delineated goal framework. Without a cohesive frame of reference, environmental education is a curricular glut—multi-faceted, unorganized, fragmented, and probably ineffective.

Although EE is widely used in non-formal contexts (e.g., zoos, museums, parks, etc.), most school-based educators have not adopted a frame of reference for EE curriculum or instruction. EE in American schools is neither theoretical, systematic, nor comprehensive. The often-made claims that a biology course deals, in part, with ecological concepts or that a particular teacher "talks about" environmental issues is not compelling evidence that environmental education is being taught.

Hungerford, Volk, and Ramsey (1990) developed a set of curriculum goals in EE to provide a sense of direction and a frame of reference for curriculum planning. These goals encompass the following four levels of cognitive knowledge and skills within a broad scope of environmental literacy:

1. Ecological foundations
2. Issue awareness
3. Investigation and evaluation
4. Issue resolution.

The first two goal levels—foundations and awareness—focus on conceptual awareness of ecological principles and of environmental issues. The latter levels include goals that deal with the development and application of skills prerequisite to investigating and evaluating issues, and to participating in the remediation of these issues.

EE, then, should prepare individuals to respond to a rapidly changing technological world, to understand contemporary world problems, and to provide the skills needed to play an effective role in the improvement and maintenance of the environment (Hungerford and Peyton, 1976). EE should also incorporate many aspects of the environment—natural, man-made, technological, social, economic, political, cultural, and aesthetic. Further, EE should emphasize and link the personal, local, national, and global actions of today with the consequences of tomorrow.

State-Level EE Initiatives

Despite environmental education's lack of status in American schools, several states have begun to exercise "top-down" leadership in establishing EE in the school curriculum. During the 1980s, Arizona, Florida, Iowa, Pennsylvania, and Wisconsin all enacted a variety of legislation that, in part, promoted EE within local school districts' curricula.

Wisconsin's initiatives, as a component of a larger statewide educational reform package, included:

- A preservice environmental educational requirement for about two-thirds of all teachers (i.e., early childhood, elementary, agriculture, science, and social studies) applying for state certification
- The development of an environmental education curriculum guide
- The creation of a school district standard requiring environmental education curriculum planning
- The creation of standards for secondary level teacher preparation programs in the environmental studies
- The establishment of a state-level environmental education board to oversee an environmental education center and an educational grants program. (Engelson, 1989).

Wisconsin uses an infusion model that requires the systematic incorporation of EE into existing district curriculum plans. To support planning at the district level, an EE curriculum guide has been developed that prescribes goals and objectives and suggests curricular and instructional strategies. Further, to a more limited extent, expertise has been made available to district planning units.

By Fall 1990, all school districts in Wisconsin had developed, adopted, and submitted curriculum plans that infuse EE into the existing curricular framework. Accountability will be determined every three years via on-site audits in which the district's written plans are compared with its educational practices. Plans are also underway to include an EE component in the statewide student assessment program.

EE in Schools—Insertion or Infusion?

School administrators and curriculum planners must face the dilemma of curricula filled with the demands of an array of discipline-based, societal-based, and learner-based needs.

How can EE curricula be reasonably framed? Can appropriate new courses be inserted into the curriculum? Can appropriate EE strategies be infused into existing curricula? Can existing curricula be appropriately modified, i.e., "environmentalized." The answer to all these questions is "yes." In fact, all three approaches might well be needed to achieve a systematic, comprehensive curricular package.

Before dealing with generic curricular factors (e.g., scope and sequence, infusion, etc.), let's review two EE instructional models built around the goal framework presented earlier. One model, the *Case Study*, was designed for infusion into existing K-12 curricula. The other model, *Issue Investigation Skill*, was designed to stand alone, requiring insertion into a grade 6-12 curriculum. These strategies represent examples of approaches that can be used by curriculum planners in "environmentalizing" the curriculum. A comparison of each approach will allow the benefits and problems associated with each to emerge.

■ **The EE Case Study Format.** The case study is a teacher-directed analysis of a particular environmental issue, an instructional method that utilizes both primary and secondary sources to deliver issue-focused information and skills to the student. In other words, original sources are, at least initially, used by the teacher to develop a foundation of knowledge concerning the issue.

Once students are oriented to the issue, the teacher provides them with the skills needed to investigate the issue on a class or small-group basis. Such a strategy could involve the students in a search for additional secondary information sources, or, it could involve a class decision concerning information needed or questions that need to be answered at the local/ community level. This could lead to instruction on the development of survey instruments (questionnaires and/or opinionnaires) and the development of a survey that the entire class would administer within the community. Primary data would then be recorded and interpreted.

Once class decisions are made concerning what should be done with respect to the issue, the time is ripe for citizenship action training and the eventual development of an action plan that may or may not be implemented, depending on decisions made by the class/teacher.

A Science-Technology-Society Case Study: Municipal Solid Waste (Ramsey, Hungerford, and Volk, 1989), a model issue instruction case study for grades 5-12, provides a model for teachers who wish to prepare case studies about issues of their choice.

The case study provides the teacher with a substantial amount of flexibility and control. The extent to which the issue is addressed is determined by the teacher, who can choose the issue, determine the instructional methods to be used and the depth to which the issue will be studied, select the content area into which the area will be infused, and determine the length of time to be spent on the case study. Ample opportunities are available for individual, large-group, or cooperative learning formats.

However, a price is paid for flexibility and control. The costs involve time, energy, and skill in putting the case study together. Most issue case studies are a "do it yourself" curriculum with the classroom teacher as the curriculum designer.

Although students can be involved in the selection of a case study, that responsibility generally rests with the teacher. So, too, does the responsibility for finding and selecting original sources such as videotapes, printed matter, guest speakers, panel members, films, field trips, or simulations. Decisions must be made about the specific learning outcomes desired, handouts must be prepared, and evaluation instruments must be designed. Developing a case study is not easy.

Another problem with the case study format relates to students' interests. The teacher cannot meet the interests of all students using the case study format. A number of students might like to investigate issues other than the one being studied by the class. This limitation is counteracted by using the issue investigation skill format.

■ **The Issue Investigation Skill Format.** The case study approach focuses on only one issue category; the issue itself is the intent of case study instruction. And, as such, the instructional activities are *issue specific*.

In contrast, the investigation skill methodology employs a broader, more generalizable approach to the process of issue investigation. The intent of the issue investigation methodology is to develop in students the capabilities (skills) in issue investigation and resolution—capabilities that can be used throughout their lives.

Like the case study approach, the investigation skill format utilizes instructional activities structured around the four issue instruction goal levels described earlier. However, unlike the case study approach, the investigation skill method defines, practices, and applies the generic knowledge and skills needed by students to independently investigate and resolve issues. This process culminates in an investigation of a science-related social issue of the student's own choosing and the development of an action plan for resolving that issue.

The investigation skill methodology for grades 6-12 has been formalized and published: *Investigating and Evaluating Environmental Issues and Actions: Skill Development Modules* (Hungerford et al., 1988). The investigation skill program is organized into a series of six modules which are interdisciplinary in nature and introduce students to the characteristics of issues, the skills needed for obtaining and processing information, the skills needed for investigating and analyzing issues, and those skills needed by responsible citizens for issue resolution. The following descriptions provide a brief overview of each module.

Module I. An Introduction to Issue Investigation

Students discriminate between events, problems, and issues. The impact of beliefs and values on science-related social issues is explored and issue analysis is introduced and practiced. The concept of "interaction," so crucial in the sciences and social studies, is also introduced, demonstrated, and applied.

Module II. The Basics of Issue Investigation

Students identify science-related social issues, write research questions, learn how to gain information from secondary sources, and learn how to compare and evaluate information sources.

Module III. Using Surveys, Opinionnaires, and Questionnaires

Students learn how to obtain information using primary methods of investigation. Initially, they learn how to develop surveys, opinionnaires, and questionnaires. Subsequently, they learn sampling techniques, how to administer data collection instruments, and how to record these data.

Module IV. Interpreting Data

Students learn how to draw conclusions, make inferences, and formulate recommendations. They also learn how to produce and interpret graphs.

Module V. Investigating an Issue

Students autonomously select and investigate a science-related social issue. This process involves the application and synthesis of the skills learned thus far.

Module VI. Issue Resolution Training

Students learn the major methods of citizenship action, analyze the effectiveness of individual versus group action, and develop issue resolution action plans. This "action plan" is evaluated against predetermined criteria to assess social, cultural, and ecological implications of citizenship actions. Finally, the action plan may be implemented at the discretion of the student.

This skill development approach provides a powerful vehicle for the investigation of a multitude of different science-related issues by students. The effectiveness of this methodology has been validated by research findings that indicated that issue investigation training fostered responsible and independent citizenship behavior in seventh and eighth grade students (Ramsey, Hungerford, and Tomera, 1981).

The investigation skill approach is probably more effective at fostering responsible citizenship behavior than the issue case study. The case study typically focuses on a single issue selected by the teacher, thus limiting exposure to an array of issues investigated by classmates and the ownership that comes with identifying and investigating one's own issue.

Most instructional methods, including the investigation skill approach, have a variety of problems and limitations. Teachers have typically found that a complete 18-week semester is needed to complete the instructional objectives in the skill development program. Thus, this type of program must be inserted into the curriculum.

Further, a variety of classroom management skills are critical in those aspects of instruction in which the teacher acts as a facilitator between resources and students in the process of investigating an array of science-related social issues. In particular, some teachers have found that it is difficult to make the transition from direct instruction to a role that demands advising and consulting. Evidently, many teachers view allowing students to independently investigate issues as an unfamiliar departure from "traditional" classroom management practice.

Consider the following stories about individuals or teams of students conducting independent investigations as a function of learning issue investigation skills in the middle school classroom.

Vignette 1. An Illinois community was engaged in deciding what combination of recreational, agricultural, commercial, industrial, and habitat usage was appropriate for a section of state-owned land adjacent to a local river. A team of middle school students assessed community residents' opinions concerning the issue. Then, using the study's findings, they developed a "master plan" for the use and development of that public land. The plan was then submitted and defended at a public hearing sponsored by the state Department of Conservation. Among the farmers, boaters, bird watchers, businessmen, and others who spoke at the hearing, the students were the only participants who presented a proposal founded on data-based decision making.

Vignette 2. Illegal dumping has become an issue in many states. In southern Illinois, a county board of commissioners received several complaints from residents concerning illegal dumping on rural roads, abandoned strip mines, and creeks. A local eighth grade student decided to determine the extent of and the characteristics associated with the county's illegal dumping activity. The student's questionnaire, along with a copy of a county map, was sent to each county township road commissioner.

Each commissioner reported the locations of illegal dump sites within his township. The student then visited each site to determine the extent of agricultural, automotive, commercial, and household wastes. A report of the findings, along with photographic evidence, was prepared and submitted to the county board of commissioners and published in the local newspaper. Further, the student used the investigation's data as the basis of a school science fair project.

Earlier we discussed how environmental education can be *infused* into the classroom. These vignettes serve as examples of products of instruction *inserted* into a middle school curriculum using the issue investigation skill strategy. The instructional examples presented above describe examples of environmental education in the classroom. However, something very important is missing: the actual planning and decision making about scope and sequence, infusion or insertion, as well as an array of other curricular and instructional questions.

Considering EE Infusion

Infusion is a relatively simple process to understand but a rather complex process to accomplish. *Simply stated, infusion refers to the integration of content and skills into existing courses to focus on that content (and/or skills) without jeopardizing the integrity of the courses themselves.* In the case of environmental education, the educator carefully analyzes existing courses for places where environmental content and associated skills could be incorporated.

A key component in the infusion process rests with the school faculty. Any comprehensive infusion strategy demands a great deal of cooperation from the staff members who will be responsible for the infused program. The faculty must be sympathetic toward the infusion and be willing to work cooperatively to build a plan for infusion and see that the plan is carried out.

A major ingredient of that "plan" must be that staff members respect the integrity of the scope and sequence in a manner that guarantees that instruction will proceed logically across content areas. Sometimes this can be accomplished by teachers working independently of others, but often it necessitates team teaching with instructors from two or more content areas working cooperatively to deliver well-thought out instruction.

If time and other resources permit, an "infusion institute" can be designed that would permit faculty members to be trained in infusion techniques and provide time for them to plan for the infusion of environmental content and skills. In addition, such an institute would allow participants to identify barriers to infusion and develop strategies for removing these barriers. This strategy will often counteract a common behavior that consists of looking for problems more diligently than looking for solutions. Human nature being what it is, excuses are far easier to come by than solutions to problems.

Some Insights into Infusion

Environmental content and skills can often be integrated into existing courses without interfering with the content and skills desired by involved faculty members.

Where can important environmental content be infused? Let us look at just a few examples and anecdotes. For example, staff members at a middle school in New Jersey were interested in implementing environmental issue instruction using a team-teaching approach (infusing issue instruction into science, language arts, and social studies).

The language arts teacher was skeptical—unsure whether this infusion would interfere with his program of skill development in the language arts. Even so, he agreed to study the components of issue investigation and respond to the challenge a day later. He came back to the group the next day and said that the language processes involved in issue instruction would meet more than 50 percent of his course objectives.

The social studies teacher, concerned that her students had an opportunity to study social problems, had no problem seeing the relationships between environmental issues and social issues, since all environmental issues have a strong social dimension. The science content was obvious.

In another instance where issue instruction was implemented in the middle school, the school librarian worked with the science teacher, assisting her with instruction in certain language skills and providing environmentally-related secondary resources for the students.

The librarian reported that she was astounded to find that the issue-focused students' research skills were much better than the skills of other students. She was also impressed with the seriousness with which those students approached their library research. The students became so skilled in using secondary sources from the library that they didn't need to be re-taught library skills in subsequent years. One would not necessarily expect this kind of an outcome from an environmental program but this is exactly what happened.

Typically, science teachers work with social studies teachers or language arts teachers to meet the needs of learners, using some form of infusion.

In other instances, teachers of home economics and agriculture request training for infusing environmental content into their subject matter areas.

Many environmentally-related issues are suitable for home economics instruction, e.g., those having to do with energy consumption and conservation, those having to do with the relationships between human reproduction and family living, issues related to environmentally-sound consumer behavior, issues related to home sanitation and disease, issues associated with toxic chemicals and food production, etc.

In agriculture, numerous environmental issues are available for infusion, e.g., issues associated with food production, soil erosion, desertification, herbicides, insecticides, livestock grazing, loss of agricultural land due to construction, etc. Courses such as home economics and agriculture can play an important part in an overall infusion of environmental education into the middle school curriculum.

Inspecting a Scope and Sequence
for Infusion Possibilities

To assist schools wanting to infuse environmental content across the curriculum, three tables were constructed that provide insight into the potential for infusing a three-year scope and sequence appropriate for middle school students. This school level was targeted because of the cognitive maturation of middle school students and the perception that the middle school curriculum is more flexible than the secondary school curriculum.

The scope and sequence begins in Year 1 with instruction focused at the discipline of ecology (Table 1). Year 2 (Table 2) focuses on environmental science and environmental health. Year 3 (Table 3) completes the sequence by focusing on environmental issue analysis, investigation, and resolution. The concepts and skills presented within the scope and sequence are tersely communicated. A complete explication of a similar scope and sequence can be found in Hungerford, Volk, and Ramsey (1990).

These tables show possibilities only. Educational needs and opportunities will vary from school to school and a given faculty may choose to infuse quite differently from what is shown in these tables.

One Last Comment

There are many opportunities for environmental education in the middle school curriculum. What about EE in the primary and intermediate elementary grades? Again, there are just as many "windows" for infusion. A number of EE curriculum packages were designed to supplement existing curriculum. Among these are *Project Learning Tree*, *Project WILD-Elemen-*

Table 1: Middle School Infusion Possibilities for Year One

Ecological Foundations and Man as an Ecological Factor

Outline Topic	SC	HE	SS	MA	LA	HO	AG
I. What Is Ecology? What Do Ecologists Do?							
A. Defining "ecology"	X						
B. The role of ecologists	X		X				X
II. Individuals, Populations, and Levels of Organization in Ecology	X						
III. The "Ecosystem Concept" Developed							
A. Importance of the concept	X						
B. Local/regional ecosystems	X						
C. Components of ecosystems	X						X
D. Ecological niches	X						X
E. Competition	X						X
F. Tolerance ranges	X						X
IV. Energy and Ecosystems							
A. The need for energy	X					X	X
B. The sun as the source	X					X	X
C. Green plants as the basis	X						X
D. Energy losses	X					X	X
E. Net primary productivity	X						X
V. Ecological Succession							
A. Succession as a natural phenomenon	X						X
B. Succession as an orderly phenomenon	X						
C. Major categories	X						X
D. A comparison of stages	X						
VI. Populations and Their Dynamics	X						X
VII. Man as an Ecological Factor							
A. Man as a powerful variable	X		X				X
B. Man as an eruptive population	X		X	X			
C. Consequences of eruptive human populations	X		X			X	X
D. Man and the world's soils			X				X
E. Man and the world's forests	X		X				X
F. Man and the world's wetlands	X		X				X
G. Man and the world's wildlife	X		X	X			
H. Critical considerations	X		X				X

Key: SC = Science; HE = Health; SS = Social Studies; MA = Math; LA = Language Arts;
HO = Home Economics; AG = Agriculture

Table 2: Middle School Infusion Possibilities for Year Two

Environmental Science & Environmental Health

Outline Topic	SC	HE	SS	MA	LA	HO	AG
I. Man: His History of Resource Consumption							
A. Early Man: hunters/gatherers			X				
B. Agricultural societies	X		X				X
C. Industrial societies	X		X				
D. Relation of population	X	X	X	X		X	X
II. Soils and Allied Problems							
A. A definition	X						X
B. Man's dependency	X						X
C. Soil formation	X						X
D. Soil erosion	X						X
E. The link between human population/soil erosion			X				X
F. Soil conservation strategies							X
III. Water and Allied Problems							
A. The world's water supply	X		X				
B. Renewing the water supply	X		X				
C. Problems with water resources	X		X				X
D. Management strategies	X		X				X
E. Water conservation	X		X			X	X
IV. Food Production and Hunger							
A. The food that feeds the world	X		X			X	X
B. Food chain energy losses	X					X	X
C. Characteristics of agricultural systems	X		X				X
D. World food problems	X	X	X			X	X
E. The green revolution	X						X
F. . . . unconventional food plants	X					X	X
G. Increasing utilization of fish	X					X	X
H. Sustainable agriculture			X				X
I. Responsibilities of the individual			X				X
V. Forest Resources							
A. Importance	X		X				
B. Short term vs long term benefits			X				
C. The world's forests			X				X
VI. Air Pollution							
A. Sources of air pollution	X		X				
B. Major pollutants	X	X					

Key: SC = Science; HE = Health; SS = Social Studies; MA = Math; LA = Language Arts;
HO = Home Economics; AG = Agriculture

Table 2: Continued

Outline Topic	SC	HE	SS	MA	LA	HO	AG
C. Impact on human health	X	X					
D. Acid precipitation	X	X					X
E. Indoor air pollution	X	X				X	
F. Ozone depletion	X	X				X	
VIII. Water Pollution							
A. Sources of surface pollution	X						X
B. Human diseases traced to		X				X	
C. Oceanic pollution		X					
D. Ground water pollution	X	X				X	X
E. Waste water treatment	X	X				X	
IX. Noise Pollution							
A. Sources and levels	X						
B. Effect of noise on humans	X	X				X	
C. Noise control	X	X	X			X	
X. Solid Waste Disposal							
A. Solid waste defined		X				X	
B. Sources of solid waste		X				X	X
C. Sources of municipal waste		X				X	
D. Affluent/nonaffluent nations			X	X			
E. Methods of municipal waste disposal		X				X	
F. Source reduction of wastes	X		X			X	X
G. Issues surrounding solid waste management	X	X	X			X	X
H. The individual			X			X	X
XI. Hazardous Waste							
A. Hazardous waste defined	X	X				X	X
B. Sources of hazardous waste	X					X	X
C. Hazardous waste disposal in the past	X					X	X
D. Hazardous waste today	X					X	X
E. Issues surrounding hazardous waste disposal	X	X				X	X
F. The individual			X			X	X
XII. Human Population Growth and Control							
A. No population can sustain limitless growth	X			X		X	
B. Human population dynamics	X		X	X		X	
C. Age structure	X		X	X			
D. Issues associated with	X		X			X	X

Key: SC = Science; HE = Health; SS = Social Studies; MA = Math; LA = Language Arts;
    HO = Home Economics; AG = Agriculture

Table 2: Continued

Outline Topic	SC	HE	SS	MA	LA	HO	AG
E. Economic development and population changes			X	X		X	
F. Advantages of family planning combined with economic development		X	X			X	
G. Immigration and population dynamics			X				
H. Birth control and population dymanics		X				X	
I. Major issues	X	X	X			X	

Key: SC = Science; HE = Health; SS = Social Studies; MA = Math; LA = Language Arts;
HO = Home Economics; AG = Agriculture

Table 3: Middle School Infusion Possibilities for Year Three

Issue Investigation and Citizenship Action Training

Outline Topic	SC	HE	SS	MA	LA	HO	AG
I. Environmental Problem Solving							
A. Human-environment interactions	X		X				
B. Quality of life vs quality of the environment	X	X	X			X	X
C. Environmental problems and issues	X	X	X			X	X
D. Issue analysis	X	X	X			X	X
E. Examples of analyzed issues	X	X	X			X	X
F. Applying issue analysis skills	X	X	X			X	X
II. Identifying Issues and Preparing Research Questions							
A. Identifying environmental issues	X	X	X			X	X
B. Identifying variables associated with environmental issues	X		X				
C. Writing research questions	X		X		X		
III. Using Secondary Sources							
A. Secondary sources of issue-related information					X		

Key: SC = Science; HE = Health; SS = Social Studies; MA = Math; LA = Language Arts;
HO = Home Economics; AG = Agriculture

Table 3: Continued

Outline Topic	SC	HE	SS	MA	LA	HO	AG
B. Processing information from secondary sources			X		X		
C. Reporting secondary source information					X		
IV. Using Primary Sources							
A. Surveys, questionnaires, and opinionnaires	X		X		X		
B. The interview					X		
C. Selecting the population	X		X	X			
D. Procedures of sampling	X		X	X			
E. Data collection strategies	X		X				
F. Developing and using instruments/ interviews	X	X	X		X	X	X
V. Interpreting Data from Environmental Issue Investigations							
A. Organizing data in data tables	X		X	X			
B. Communicating data by graphing	X		X	X			
C. Interpreting data	X		X		X		
D. Applying data interpreting skills to issue-related data sets	X	X	X			X	X
VI. The Independent Investigation of a Student-Selected Environmental Issue							
A. Selecting an issue	X	X	X		X	X	X
B. Writing research questions	X	X	X		X	X	X
C. Collecting secondary information			X		X		
D. Collecting primary information	X	X	X	X	X	X	X
E. Issue analysis/data interpretation	X		X	X	X		
F. Communication of results					X		
VII. Issue Resolution: Skills and Application							
A. Citizenship responses to issues and their effects	X	X	X			X	X
B. Principles of citizenship action			X				
C. Methods of citizenship action			X			X	X
D. Individual vs group action		X	X			X	X
E. Guidelines for decision making	X	X	X			X	X
F. Applying issue resolution skills		X	X	X		X	X

Key: SC = Science; HE = Health; SS = Social Studies; MA = Math; LA = Language Arts; HO = Home Economics; AG = Agriculture *tary*, and *NatureScope*—all of which provide interdisciplinary activities and infusion ideas.

What about the discipline-focused secondary school? *Project WILD-Secondary* is widely used as a curriculum supplement in high school science courses. Further, upper level biology, chemistry, and physics courses present excellent opportunities for the infusion of teacher-developed case studies. For example, an acid rain case study (constructed in congruence with the EE goal hierarchy) might follow a "acids" unit in a chemistry course.

But thoughtful curriculum planners know that episodic treatments only in certain courses must be avoided. Environmental education, in order to achieve its goals, must be systematically constructed and theoretically valid.

Wisconsin (Engelson, 1989) has proposed the following infusion framework (Figure 1) to ensure systemwide planning for that state's curriculum planners:

Figure 1
Wisconsin's EE Curriculum Model

Grade Level Range	Subgoals: Major Emphasis	Subgoals: Minor Emphasis
K-3	Awareness Attitudes and Values	Knowledge Citizen Action Skills Citizen Action Experience
3-6	Knowledge Attitudes and Values	Awareness Citizen Action Skills Citizen Action Experience
6-9	Knowledge Citizen Action Skills Attitudes and Experience	Awareness Citizen Action Experience
9-12	Citizen Action Skills Citizen Action Experience Attitudes and Experience	Awareness Knowledge

References

Childress, R.B. "Public School Environmental Education Curricula: A National Profile." *Journal of Environmental Education* 3(1978): 2-12

"Conference Declaration on Environmental Education." *Convergence* 4(1977): 70-71.

Engelson, D.R. *A Guide to Curriculum Planning in Environmental Education*. Madison, Wis.: Wisconsin Department of Public Instruction, 1989.

————. "Recent Wisconsin Initiatives in Environmental Education." In *Working Together To Educate About the Environment*. Troy, Ohio: North American Association for Environmental Education, 1989.

Hungerford, H.R.; Litherland, R.A.; Peyton, R.B.; Ramsey, J.M.; and Volk, T.L. *Investigating and Evaluating Environmental Issues and Actions: Skill Development Modules*. Champaign, Ill.: Stipes Publishing, 1988.

Hungerford, H.R., and Peyton, R.B. *Teaching Environmental Education*. Portland, Maine: J. Weston Walch, 1976.

Hungerford, H.R.; Volk, T.L.; and Ramsey, J.M. *A Prototype Environmental Education Curriculum for the Middle School*. Paris: UNESCO/UNEP, 1990.

Ramsey, J.M., and Hungerford, H.R. "Effects of Issue Investigation and Action Training on Characteristics Associated with Environmental Behavior in Seventh Grade Students." *Journal of Environmental Education* 1(1989): 26-30.

————. "So . . . You Want to Teach Issues?" *Contemporary Education* 3(1989): 137-42.

Ramsey, J.M.; Hungerford, H.R.; and Tomera, A.N. "Effects of Environmental Action and Environmental Case Study Instruction on the Overt Environmental Behavior of Eighth Grade Students." *Journal of Environmental Education* 1(1981): 24-29.

Ramsey, J.M.; Hungerford, H.R.; and Volk, T.L. *A Science-Technology-Society Case Study: Municipal Solid Waste*. Champaign, Ill.: Stipes Publishing, 1989.

————. "Analyzing the Issues of STS." *The Science Teacher* 3(1983): 60-63.

Chapter 9

Can We Move Writing Across the Curriculum?

Margaret Earley

To English/language arts educators and researchers, the reasons to promote writing across the curriculum are obvious. To their colleagues in other disciplines, however, the reasons may not be so immediately compelling. Even when content teachers accept the desirability of the goal, they often see little hope for implementing it.

How can secondary school principals help teachers achieve a goal that many are convinced is worthy but unattainable? First, let's review why developing students' literacy should be every teacher's concern in grades 6-12. Then we'll consider the forces working against this laudable goal and look for ways these forces can be counteracted by principals who believe that teaching students to read, write, and think is an all-school priority.

Why We Want Writing Across the Curriculum

We have learned much about writing and the teaching of writing in the past 20 years. Reduced to simple propositions, much of what we are learning about writing processes seems unarguable. For example, most people—principals, teachers, students, parents, adults generally—could identify with the "we" in the following statements:
- We cannot develop ease in writing unless we write frequently.
- We learn what we know, or don't know, about a topic when we try to put that knowledge into writing.
- One real reason for writing is to communicate what we know to persons who are interested in our perceptions.
- Writing requires us to sort out hazy notions so we state our ideas clearly enough for others to comprehend them.

- We write differently—use different processes—depending on what we are writing.
- On some days, on some topics, we write more easily and more successfully than on others. Because writing ability is not a unitary thing, not an abstraction, it is not easy to measure.

If educators agree that these propositions fit their own experiences as writers and learners, they can use them to guide instructional practices and curriculum development. In short, what we know about the need for practice, purpose, audience, and feedback in the development of ease in writing tells us that students need more opportunities to write than they can get in English classes alone. They need feedback from teachers and peers *as they write*.

Merely writing more papers for teachers' grades is insufficient. And after interaction with responsive peers, students need an "unseen audience" as often as possible to make real the reason for writing in the first place. Since writing is a way of learning, a way of knowing, students should use it frequently in all disciplines where they are expected to assimilate ideas and make them their own.

Why Progress Is Slow

So the ideal curriculum in secondary schools makes writing and reading foundational. Why isn't it happening in more schools? In spite of 50 years of exhortation, in spite of 20 years of sound research on psycholinguistic processes, valid reports on instruction and achievement in writing are dismal (Applebee et al., 1990). Impressions of illiteracy are rampant among business leaders who hire our high school graduates and among college professors who try to further educate them.

Of the many reasons that can be cited for slow progress in implementing writing across the curriculum, perhaps the most intractable is the faculty/student ratio in grades 6 to 12. Just as serious is content teachers' lack of understanding that writing is a means of learning as well as a manifestation of what is known, and their consequent view that they are being asked to add one more requirement to an already overloaded curriculum.

Even when teachers deepen their understanding of writing process and pedagogy, they are often frustrated in their attempts to reform the teaching of writing in their own classrooms, to say nothing of spreading enlightened writing instruction to colleagues' classrooms. They say they have too many students, too much else to teach in too-brief class periods, state assessments to prepare for, students who are turned off to writing, and too many cocurricular chores to perform. Their enthusiasm wilts in the realities of the school year.

When we urge writing across the curriculum, we are really asking for fundamental reform in the way schools are organized. We are asking for school settings where teachers can serve as coaches to students who are learning through writing and reading. We are asking for teachers who see themselves in different relationships to learners and to subject matter than they themselves have ever experienced as students. We are asking for teachers who are willing to learn new roles and who have the time to do so. We are asking for summer institutes for all content teachers, not just English teachers, and for institutes that are centered on more than writing and writing instruction.

A second emphasis must be on content teachers' rethinking of the pedagogy of their disciplines. They must come up with instructional strategies including assignments, projects, and examination questions that enable students to see how writing enhances learning in science, mathematics, history, and other disciplines. As teachers become convinced of the usefulness of writing assignments in promoting learning in their own subjects, they will be motivated to find ways of handling the paper load, which is to say ways of responding to writing and evaluating learning.

None of this will be easy. At first it will seem to teachers that time is the big inhibiting factor. Where will the history teacher with 125 students find time to read his/her output once she has aroused their enthusiasm for writing like historians, for gathering and reporting information for their peers, for writing journals typical of persons and events in the period they are studying?

Time is a major problem because of unrealistic faculty/student ratio, but it is also a result of cutting the curriculum into 45-50 minute segments. Even if teachers were responsible for coaching and monitoring fewer students, if schedules remain unchanged, students will still be frustrated by having too little time to pursue an idea and capture it on paper (or film or in an oral report to classmates).

Nevertheless, teachers wrestling with the time factor will soon realize that how they use time depends on what they believe about teaching. Those who see teaching primarily as sharing with students their knowledge of a respected, essential subject will have a bred-in-the-bone need to assign, direct, and evaluate students' learning. They will feel compelled to read and evaluate every paper, and when the paperload overwhelms them, they will resort to objective tests, short-answer quizzes, estimates based on students' oral responses, and to even less reliable assessments.

This view of teaching as dispensing and examining knowledge is the norm. As such, it won't be easily modified, even slightly. Not only will teachers resist, but parents, administrators, and students will argue that teachers must be masters and examiners. Moreover, the ways that teachers act on this belief have become habitual, and habits are hard to erase even when the spirit is willing.

To come out from behind the lectern, to listen to students, to coach them, to get them to feel responsible for their own and each other's learning, to let students find and correct their own mistakes—all this requires not only conviction and courage but the breaking of teacherly habits. Teachers who decide to change their styles need support systems that operate over the long haul just as anyone kicking a habit needs sustaining help.

What Administrators Can Do

Principals engaged in school improvement see writing across the curriculum as a piece of the total design. Learning from and with their faculty, they understand where their colleagues stand with respect to the issues surrounding writing instruction. If you are a school leader of this kind, you will examine the priorities and decide on the best starting points. No one else, certainly no one from outside your school, can offer a blueprint for change.

But if you don't know your teachers' ingrained and maybe as-yet inarticulate beliefs about writing and the teaching of writing, that's the place to begin. Indeed, you may not be sure of your own convictions in this matter. One way to find out is to take a workshop on writing. School districts have run such workshops for administrators on the hunch that they could improve the writing skills they need on the job while at the same time understanding writers' processes and instructional strategies that would benefit students.

Some principals enroll with their teachers in National Writing Project institutes that are offered every summer within reasonable distance of most schools in this country. If commitments of this kind are impractical, you can at least talk with knowledgeable English teachers on your own staff or in feeder schools, maybe in another community or at a nearby university.

The next step will be convening faculty seminars to explore teachers' beliefs about language and language instrucion. This will take time. Teachers should meet in small enough groups so they can talk freely and frankly. They should have leaders who know how to draw them out, who are sensitive to the issues. If there is not full and frank discussion, misapprehensions will persist, such as the one that equates teaching writing with correcting surface errors.

From these seminars you will identify teachers who should be given opportunities to study in summer institutes, returning to conduct sessions with their colleagues that will lead to experimenting with content-related writing assignments, collaborative writing groups, and ways to evaluate learning.

Of course, the assumption is that your faculty members see reasons for spending precious time articulating beliefs about writing. Chances are they need not only time, but motivation. You may need first to stimulate concern by inviting local business leaders to describe their need for employees who can communicate. You can also bring back recent graduates to describe their struggles with academic writing in college. Business leaders may be ready to form partnerships with your teachers to investigate problems and solutions. Such partnerships can often buy time for teachers to study, to do research, to experiment with new teaching strategies, to make the transition, where appropriate, to teacher-as-coach.

School improvement grants, whether from businesses, private foundations, or public sources, are probably necessary (though insufficient in and of themselves) for moving faculties beyond talking to doing. Instances can be cited, of course, to prove the power of the enthusiastic teacher to achieve small miracles in her own classes and to influence other teachers as well (Leopold and Jenkinson, 1988). But such instances have minimal effect on improving writing and learning across the nation. And that is the goal we are considering here.

Relating to Reading Instruction

It would be a rare secondary school that had made no efforts in recent decades to involve all content teachers in improving students' reading and, to some extent, writing. In the foregoing discussion, we don't mean to imply that principals must start from square one. On the contrary, principals must take into account not only what is happening now in literacy education, but what has been its history in their school. For instance, do teacher recognize the difference between remedial and developmental emphases? Do they assume "remediation" as the practical approach? How do the rest of the faculty members perceive teachers who are providing remedial services? Are they expected to take care of all the problems of literacy education and let content teachers get on with *their* work?

If there has been a great push for reading across the curriculum, how has it fared? How do all teachers interpret their contributions to reading instruction? If there has been an intelligent and concerted effort on study skills, content teachers may have already gone a long way toward moving writing across the curriculum.

In many middle schools, students take reading as a class in addition to language arts. Does one teacher teach both classes? If so, what kinds of integration take place? If not, how does the reading teacher collaborate with the language arts teacher? Do these teachers try to teach content area study skills in lieu of the content teachers' doing what they should be able to do better than a generalist?

In many high schools, reading resource teachers have been added to work with content teachers, replacing earlier remedial approaches and classes like Reading II, study skills, or speed reading. Their roles should be continuously changing as new faculty come on board, different student needs are identified, and the whole question of support services is reviewed in the drive for lower faculty-student ratios.

Reading specialists can be central to writing across the curriculum since, in best case scenarios, they already have the ear of the content teacher. But it is essential that reading specialists truly understand what is known about writing processes. They may accept labels like "writing to learn," "process writing," and "writing is rewriting" without fully appreciating the concepts behind them. They may have read many articles and attended many sessions at local and national conferences on relationships between reading and writing; even so, they also need the experience of a summer institute that requires them to explore processes, keep journals, write to express themselves, and write to learn.

From these experiences they will be better able to wrestle with issues like the proper balance between expressive and academic writing, the merits of Standard Written English, how whole language approaches need to be modified as students mature and curricula become more demanding. They will continue to worry, and rightly, about the balances between reading and writing in terms of students' time and faculty's emphasis.

Principals wishing to renew faculty efforts in literacy instruction should consult first with the experts on their staff: the English teachers and the reading personnel. If great rapport does not already exist between these two groups, an important first aim will be to encourage them to exchange expertise and maintain respect for both traditions.

Another early convening of experts should bring together the elementary, middle school, and senior high school reading coordinators and principals to explore current attitudes and future plans vis-à-vis whole language approaches, basal reading programs, basic skills "requirements," reading in the content areas, and the relationships within and among specialists in the system.

The principal needs the help of all these people, and they need the principal's active interest in what is, after all, their reason for being. Interest here means finding money to support staff development, working with the community, arranging school events to emphasize literacy, defining the place for writing across the curriculum in the total school improvement plan. It means commitment for the long run, and that means including in the long-range planning provisions for changes in personnel, especially a change in leadership.

What Administrators Can Do Beyond Their Schools

We have emphasized that writing across the curriculum will be achieved school by school. Different patterns will emerge, dictated by particular circumstances; for example, the community setting, relationships that have been or can be built with parents, the sophistication of the faculty with respect to literacy, the previous school experiences of the students, their achievements and expectations. Because there is no one best way to achieve a language-based curriculum, school leaders must find their own ways. But there are at least two important actions to be taken beyond individual schools.

1. Teacher Education. School administrators influence how teachers are prepared by:
- The criteria they adhere to in hiring new teachers
- How they support beginning teachers and help them to develop their beliefs about teaching
- The feedback they give back to teacher training officials
- The settings they provide for the student teaching phase of teacher preparation.

For too many years, teacher educators have been caught in the dilemma of whether to prepare teachers for schools as they are or schools as they ought to be. Many beginning teachers who have learned to coach individuals and to manage cooperative learning groups find no opportunities to do so; many who have not learned to use textbooks wisely and well are expected to do so.

Teacher educators must have principals' input in resolving their classic dilemma, and both groups should seek time for the needed dialog. An important purpose of such exchanges is to sort out what kinds of experiences are appropriately preservice and what kinds of continuing education are primarily the principal's responsibility.

In the meantime, principals inform teacher educators indirectly by the way they interview candidates. If you want to push writing across the curriculum, find out what applicants know about writing processes and instruction. Ask them, for example, *why* they might require students to write several drafts or how they would get students to write for each other, or what kinds of writing assignments they might make and how they would evaluate them.

If candidates' answers suggest they are not being well prepared for teaching writing across the curriculum, you should raise questions with teacher educators responsible for various subject fields.

2. Assessment. A well-worn excuse for not incorporating reading and writing in content areas is that state assessments and other instruments of "accountability" measure knowledge, that is, product, not process. Even in measures of reading and writing, the emphasis is on product and on bits and pieces of language rather than on the process of making meaning either as comprehension or composition. As a result, some English teachers say they can't require as much writing as they know they should because they must drill students on grammar and usage for "the state test."

Measuring achievement in reading and writing is a complicated task, one that challenges psychometricians and psycholinguists. Results of writing assessments such as those of the National Assessment of Educational Progress are criticized for measuring timed writing on assigned topics (not authentic writing) and ignoring research that shows the influence of subject and situation. Some critics say that inadequate testing procedures account for the reported low achievement in writing in the nation's secondary schools in spite of nearly two decades of re-educating thousands of teachers in process approaches. For more accurate assessment of progress, we need new ways of measuring both process and product.

Portfolio assessment has been suggested to account for long-term growth, the influence of topics and situations, and the contrasts between writing on demand and writing developed over time from the students' self-selected topics. Several state testing programs are experimenting with portfolio assessments and with new measures of reading comprehension that tap process as well as product.

As principals work with reading and writing teachers for improved assessments, they can also interpret for all teachers and parents the limitations of present measures. They can lead their faculties in considering how they can best evaluate how well students are learning.

Conclusion

In answer to the question posed in the title, we have proposed that principals recognize writing across the curriculum as one piece in a larger plan for improving their school's services to students; that they set priorities according to their particular school's mixture of faculty, students, and community interests; that they deepen their own understanding of writing processes and pedagogy and lead their faculties to do so; and that, realizing how slowly teachers' beliefs emerge and change, they prepare for a long road ahead.

There are reasons for guarded optimism, however. Enthusiasm for whole language approaches is spreading upward from the primary schools, and in increasing numbers, secondary school content teachers expect to teach study skills. Teachers are reexamining their roles. We are looking again at restructuring secondary schools. It's not unreasonable to expect the goal of a language-based curriculum to become a reality.

References

Applebee, A.N., Langer, J.A., et al. *Learning To Write in Our Nation's Schools: Instruction and Achievement in 1988 in Grades 4, 8, and 12*. Princeton, N.J.: National Assessment of Educational Progress, 1990.

Leopold, A.H., and Jenkinson, E.B. "The Cummins Engine Foundation Writing Project: A Cooperative Venture with Public Schools." *Phi Delta Kappan*, June 1988. Note: This issue of the *Kappan* features writing across the curriculum, and is worth your attention.

Chapter 10

Some Common Threads of the Interdisciplinary Curriculum

John M. Jenkins

In an information society, power falls to those persons who are best able to acquire and apply knowledge. It is the responsibility of schools to produce graduates who are able to take their places in this society and make a contribution. How can secondary schools best be organized to meet this responsibility?

This publication has examined an old idea whose time ostensibly has arrived. The notion of integrated subject matter is not new. High school courses like American studies and humanities acknowledge the value of seeing relationships in content.

The notion of a core curriculum that integrated language arts with social studies and sometimes science at the junior high school level was popular in a number of school districts in the 1950s, while more innovative core curriculum efforts organized the school program around themes or problems rather than single subject matter disciplines.

Today, in light of the global economic competition that finds the United States lagging behind in international industrial markets, a call has been sounded by a coalition of business and education leaders to address the idea of a core curriculum in contemporary terms.

The most striking difference between this rebirth of integrated curriculum and the past is the realization that all knowledge is in some way interrelated, and that learning can be made more efficient through a process that recognizes these interrelationships. If "less is more," as Ted Sizer has suggested in *Horace's Compromise*, then taking a new look at curriculum with a focus on reducing the number of separate but related subjects seems appropriate and necessary.

Because of the knowledge explosion it is impossible to learn all there is to know in any one discipline. Organizing the school curriculum around major themes, ideas, and problems may not only be more sensible from the point of view of student learning, but also from the point of view of survival.

The introductory chapter by Daniel Tanner provides the historical context for interdisciplinary curriculum. The chapters that follow describe a number of middle and high school programs in the planning stages or in progress that are designed to bridge the gap between the traditional subjects and to make schooling more relevant to the student clientele.

In reading these accounts, several common threads are suggested irrespective of school level or subject area. These common threads can provide direction for the school practitioner in planning and implementing interdisciplinary curriculum and instruction.

- *Teaming:* Bridging the "gaps" between subjects seems best accomplished when teams of teachers with different subject matter specialties plan together for instruction. What to teach and when to teach it is decided by the team within district and state frameworks.

  In getting started, interdisciplinary teams should be flexible, blending individual "turn teaching" with truly integrated instruction. Teachers should take on a variety of roles. Research results consistently show the value of collaborative planning for instruction, yet, much of what happens in the secondary schools supports only individual activity.

- *Flexible Scheduling:* Interdisciplinary teaching requires that teachers be given time to plan together for instruction. The importance of planning cannot be overstated. *Blocks of time* over which teachers have a measure of control allow for the kind of flexibility in which all students assigned to a team can be brought together for a particular experience or in which varying group sizes can be arranged to match the learning activity with the characteristics of specific students.

  When the budget allows for the employment of a resource teacher to work with a team or differentiated staff, additional flexibility is possible. The lowering of the adult-student ratio facilitates a more personalized approach to education.

  No matter what scheduling pattern evolves, one point is clear: common planning time for the team is essential. If integrated teaching is to occur, the teachers charged with that responsibility must be given the time to plan and work together.

- *Different Roles for Teachers:* In interdisciplinary teaching, the teachers are both specialists and generalists. As specialists, they bring the perspective of their disciplines to bear upon a problem or a theme. As generalists, they stand back from their areas of expertise to look for ways to integrate two or three different disciplines. Sometimes, they even take responsibility for teaching subjects other than their own specialties.

The isolation and territoriality characteristic of the traditional subject-centered school is replaced with a camaraderie among members of a team that transcends individual personalities and uses the strengths of the team members advantageously to improve instruction for all students. Longer time periods enable the teachers to work more personally with students and to shift their focus from subject matter to the interaction of pedagogy and curriculum in individual students. In a phrase, teaching becomes more student-centered.

- *Support from the Principal.* Significant school changes require the support and leadership of the principal. Providing time in the schedule for teaching teams to plan is accomplished only when the principal builds a schedule that facilitates this arrangement. Selecting the make-up of teams and finding the necessary time for the teams to plan initially are the responsibility of the principal.

Sometimes the support given to teachers who are working on new programs may cause other teachers to view them negatively. The in-group/out-group phenomenon can cause stress and strain among the faculty. The principal must involve as many faculty members as possible in new undertakings to reduce the negative impact of differential treatment. In the final anaysis, however, some conflict may be unavoidable.

The principal must look for ways to employ teachers in the summer so they have time to plan new directions and reflect on where they have been. Capital investment in planning is money well-spent. It gives teachers the uninterrupted time they need to move forward and lets them know they have the principal's support.

- *Commitment:* Teachers and administrators must be committed to the change process. They must be willing to invest hours "beyond the call of duty." Research shows that the faculty and administration in the more effective schools share a common vision. Implementing an interdisciplinary program effectively requires a similar vision.

The highs and lows that accompany any kind of change will likely occur; an ability to overcome obstacles and learn from experience is a necessity.

Ancillary Threads

Two ancillary threads accompany the five common threads detailed above and are facilitated when a school begins to restructure curriculum through some form of subject integration.

First, the notion of curriculum is redefined so all students are assured of a common core of learning. This common core is derived by examining what is currently taught and defining it in terms of essential learnings and desirable learnings. The essential learnings are considerably less than what has traditionally been the case, leaving opportunities for more students to explore areas of individual interest.

Along with the common core of learnings, one finds a new perspective on student evaluation that emphasizes real learning in real situations. When the focus of instruction becomes more personal, then how a student can best present what he or she has learned becomes extremely important.

The Denouement

Ultimately, learning involves the integration of new knowledge with previously developed knowledge. How knowledge is developed very often determines how it will be utilized in the future and under what circumstances. Effective learners are much better at integrating new knowledge with old and much better at relating knowledge intelligently to new situations.

If the real measure of whether something has been learned is determined by the ability to apply knowledge and skills to problems, then learners who are able to see relationships among knowledge bases are more flexible in their problem solving. They are more knowledgeable and hence have more working power at their command.

Creative problem-solvers simultaneously see a larger picture along with the elements that compose the picture. They see both the forest and the trees. Assuming that these are the kinds of people we hope to develop as a result of schooling, then integrated teaching would appear to be the best approach. By its very nature, it broadens the scope of the knowledge base and affords students an opportunity to see the world with greater vision and understanding.